*T*o

_____

*F*rom

_____

365 DAY BRIGHTENERS

God's
CELEBRATING
Grace

365 Day Brighteners™ *Celebrating God's Grace*

© 2003 DaySpring Cards, Inc.
Publsihed by Garborg's®,
a brand of DaySpring Cards, Inc.
Siloam Springs, Arkansas

Scripture references are from the following sources:
The HOLY BIBLE, NEW INTERNATIONAL VERSION®
(NIV)® © 1973, 1978, 1984 by International Bible Society.
Used by permission of Zondervan Publishing House.
THE MESSAGE © Eugene H. Peterson 1993, 1994, 1995.
Used by permission of NavPress Publishing Group. All rights
reserved. The Living Bible (TLB) © 1971. Used by permission of
Tyndale House Publishers, Inc., Wheaton, Illinois 60189.

Except for Scripture verses, references to men and
masculine pronouns have been replaced with "people,"
"women," and gender-neutral or feminine pronouns.

ISBN 1-58061-735-2   Printed in China

365 DAY
BRIGHTENERS

God's
CELEBRATING
Grace

GARBORG'S®

because every day is a gift

*G*od guides us, despite our uncertainties
and our vagueness, even through our failings
and mistakes.... He leads us step by step,
from event to event. Only afterwards, as we
look back over the way we have come...do we
experience the feeling of having been led
without knowing it, the feeling that God
has mysteriously guided us.

PAUL TOURNIER

J a n u a r y 1

January 2

I look up and try to understand
that our solar system is a tiny pinprick in
that great river of stars.... The truth I hold to
is that it is all God's, joyfully created,
and that it is good.

MADELEINE L'ENGLE

$\mathcal{S}$omething deep in all
of us yearns for God's beauty,
and we can find it
no matter where we are.

· SUE MONK KIDD ·

J a n u a r y 3

January 4

*W*e are always in the
presence of God.... There is never
a nonsacred moment! His presence
never diminishes. Our awareness
of His presence may falter, but the
reality of His presence never changes.

MAX LUCADO

*L*ife is a promise,

fulfill it.

MOTHER TERESA

January 5

January 6

"For I know the plans I have
for you," declares the Lord,
"plans to prosper you and not
to harm you, plans to give
you hope and a future."

JEREMIAH 29:11 NIV

*G*od is every moment totally
aware of each one of us.
Totally aware in intense concentration
and love.... No man passes through
any area of life, happy or tragic,
without the attention of God with Him.

EUGENIA PRICE

January 7

January 8

Much of what is sacred
is hidden in the ordinary, everyday
moments of our lives. To see something
of the sacred in those moments
takes slowing down so we can live
our lives more reflectively.

KEN GIRE

*G*od wants us to be present
where we are. He invites us to see
and to hear what is around us and,
through it all, to discern
the footprints of the Holy.

RICHARD J. FOSTER

January 9

January 10

*J*ust to be is a blessing.

Just to live is holy.

ABRAHAM JOSHUA HESCHEL

*I*f you don't know what you're doing,
pray to the Father. He loves to help.
You'll get his help, and won't be
condescended to when you ask for it.
Ask boldly, believingly, without
a second thought.

JAMES 1:5-6 THE MESSAGE

January 11

January 12

Life is so full of meaning
and purpose, so full of beauty,
beneath its covering,
that you will find that earth
but cloaks your heaven.

FRA GIOVANNI

I am convinced
beyond a shadow of any doubt
that the most valuable pursuit
we can embark upon
is to know God.

KAY ARTHUR

January 13

January 14

Lord, I feel like a mouse in a treadmill.
Rushing around, faster and faster.
Getting nowhere...
Lord, it's at times like this that
I need you most.
Yet you seem so far away.
Why, Lord? Where have you gone?
Then I hear it, the quiet voice......
be still and know that I am.
You are near.
You have been all the time.

EDDIE ASKEW

*Y*ou are God's created beauty and the focus of His affection and delight.

JANET L. WEAVER SMITH

January 15

January 16

I love the Lord because
he hears my prayers and answers them.
Because he bends down and listens,
I will pray as long as I breathe!

PSALM 116:1–2 TLB

$\mathcal{W}$e are never more fulfilled
than when our longing for God
is met by His presence in our lives.

BILLY GRAHAM

January 17

January 18

For the God who fills human hunger
is at the same time the Unknown,
the Stranger. Only His absence–presence
allows a person to be oneself.

JEAN SULIVAN

*L*ive for today but hold your hands
open to tomorrow. Anticipate the future
and its changes with joy. There is a seed
of God's love in every event, every
circumstance, every unpleasant situation
in which you may find yourself.

BARBARA JOHNSON

January 19

January 20

God's creation cannot subsist
without God's abundant grace.
God has given human beings
the sacred responsibility of
mediating God's grace.

VIGEN GUROIAN

I have loved you with
an everlasting love;
therefore I have continued
my faithfulness to you.

JEREMIAH 31:3 NRSV

January 21

January 22

The Lord's chief desire is to reveal Himself to you and, in order for Him to do that, He gives you abundant grace. The Lord gives you the experience of enjoying His presence. He touches you, and His touch is so delightful that, more than ever, you are drawn inwardly to Him.

MADAME JEAN GUYON

$\mathcal{T}$he God who created, names,
and numbers the stars in the heavens
also numbers the hairs of my head....
He pays attention to very big things
and to very small ones. What matters
to me matters to Him, and that
changes my life.

ELISABETH ELLIOT

January 23

January 24

*S*now is falling outside my
study window.... I see nature once
more playing endless variations
in design and beauty.... In such simple
yet eloquent ways, I am reminded that
God is personal, revealing Himself
continuously in the finite.

JUDITH C. LECHMAN

*I*n a special way, human beings...
being made in the image of God,
only become real human beings, are only
able to grow and thrive as human beings,
as they also yearn for God.

ROBERTA BONDI

January 25

January 26

Steep yourself in God-reality,
God-initiative, God-provisions.
You'll find all your everyday human
concerns will be met. Don't be afraid of
missing out. You're my dearest friends!
The Father wants to give you
the very kingdom itself.

LUKE 12:28 THE MESSAGE

*A*ll God's glory and beauty
come from within, and there
He delights to dwell.
His visits there are frequent,
His conversation sweet,
His comforts refreshing,
His peace passing all understanding.

THOMAS À KEMPIS

J a n u a r y 27

January 28

If there is a God who
speaks anywhere, surely He speaks here:
through waking up and working,
through going away and coming back again,
through people you read and books you meet,
through falling asleep in the dark.

FREDERICK BUECHNER

*G*race means that God

already loves us as much

as an infinite God can

possibly love.

PHILIP YANCEY

January 29

January 30

I will let God's peace infuse every part of today. As the chaos swirls and life's demands pull at me on all sides, I will breathe in God's peace that surpasses all understanding. He has promised that He would set within me a peace too deeply planted to be affected by unexpected or exhausting demands.

*F*or the Spirit of God
has made me, and the breath
of the Almighty gives me life.

JOB 33:4 TLB

J a n u a r y 31

February 1

God is infinite in His simplicity
and simple in His infinity.
Therefore He is everywhere and is
everywhere complete. He is everywhere
on account of His infinity, and is everywhere
complete on account of His simplicity.

MEISTER ECKHART

I will remember that when
I give Him my heart, God chooses to live
within me—body and soul. And I know
He really is as close as breathing,
His very Spirit inside of me.

February 2

February 3

With God there is always more unfolding, that which we can glimpse of the divine is always exactly enough, and never enough.

KATHLEEN NORRIS

We have been in God's thought
from all eternity, and in His creative love,
His attention never leaves us.

MICHAEL QUOIST

February 4

February 5

Deep calls to deep in the roar
of your waterfalls; all your waves and
breakers have swept over me.
By day the Lord directs his love, at night
his song is with me—a prayer to
the God of my life.

PSALM 42:7–8 NIV

𝒫atience is more than a virtue
for long lines and slow waiters.
Patience is the red carpet upon
which God's grace approaches us.

MAX LUCADO

February 6

February 7

*T*onight I will sleep beneath Your feet,
O Lord of the mountains and valleys, ruler of
the trees and vines. I will rest in Your love, with
You protecting me as a father protects his
children, with You watching over me as
a mother watches over her children.
Then tomorrow the sun will rise and I will
not know where I am; but I know that
You will guide my footsteps.

ROBERT VAN DE WEYER

*I*t is not objective proof of God's existence that we want but the experience of God's presence. That is the miracle we are really after, and that is also, I think, the miracle that we really get.

FREDERICK BUECHNER

February 8

February 9

The greatest honor we can give
God is to live gladly because of
the knowledge of His love.

JULIAN OF NORWICH

$\mathcal{B}$e content with who you are,
and don't put on airs. God's strong hand
is on you; he'll promote you at
the right time. Live carefree before God;
he is most careful with you.

1 PETER 5:6–7 THE MESSAGE

February 10

February 11

*N*otice words of compassion.
Seek out deeds of kindness.
These are like the doves from heaven,
pointing out to you who are the ones
blessed with inner grace and beauty.

CHRISTOPHER DE VINCK

$\mathcal{A}$n infinite God can give all
of Himself to each of His children.
He does not distribute Himself that
each may have a part, but to each one
He gives all of Himself as fully as
if there were no others.

A. W. TOZER

February 12

February 13

*H*e made you so you could
share in His creation,
could love and laugh and know Him.

TED GRIFFEN

$\mathcal{G}$od loves and cares for us,
even to the least event and
smallest need of life.

HENRY EDWARD MANNING

February 14

February 15

For though we have never
yet seen God, when we love each other
God lives in us and his love within
us grows ever stronger.

1 JOHN 4:12 TLB

*T*he overflowing life does
not just happen. It is only as our own
deep thirst is quenched, only as we are filled
ourselves, that we can be channels through
which His overflow reaches other lives.

GRACE STRICKER DAWSON

February 16

February 17

$\mathscr{P}$eople see God every day.
They just don't recognize Him.

PEARL BAILEY

$\mathcal{A}$lthough it be good to think
upon the kindness of God, and to love
Him and worship Him for it;
yet it is far better to gaze upon the pure
essence of Him and to love Him and
worship Him for Himself.

February 18

February 19

The direct experience of God
is grace indeed, and basically there is
no one to whom it is refused.

IGNATIUS OF LOYOLA

*T*hose who hope in the Lord
will renew their strength.
They will soar on wings like eagles;
they will run and not grow weary,
they will walk and not be faint.

ISAIAH 40:31 NIV

February 20

February 21

 od is not in the vastness of greatness.

He is hid in the vastness of smallness.

He is not in the general.

He is in the particular.

PEARL S. BUCK

$\mathcal{G}$od possesses infinite knowledge
and an awareness which is uniquely His.
At all times, even in the midst of any type
of suffering, I can realize that He knows,
loves, watches, understands, and more
than that, He has a purpose.

BILLY GRAHAM

February 22

February 23

God cannot give us a
happiness and peace apart from
Himself, because it is not there.
There is no such thing.

C. S. LEWIS

*G*od reads the secrets of the heart.
God reads its most intimate feelings,
even those which we are not aware of.

JEAN–NICHOLAS GROU

February 24

February 25

What happens when we live God's way? He brings gifts into our lives, much the same way that fruit appears in an orchard—things like affection for others, exuberance about life, serenity. We develop a willingness to stick with things, a sense of compassion in the heart, and a conviction that a basic holiness permeates things and people.

GALATIANS 5:22–23 THE MESSAGE

*T*he more I study
nature, the more I am
amazed at the Creator.

LOUIS PASTEUR

February 26

February 27

*F*eel! touch and see
how gracious the Lord is!
Taste, hear, smell, feel and see
how gracious the Lord is!

MADELEINE L'ENGLE

*I*t's usually through our hard times, the unexpected and not–according–to–plan times, that we experience God in more intimate ways. We discover an unquenchable longing to know Him more. It's a passion that isn't concerned that life fall within certain predictable lines, but a passion that pursues God and knows He is relentless in His pursuit of each one of us.

February 28

February 29

*I*n waiting we begin to get in touch
with the rhythms of life—stillness and action,
listening and decision. They are the
rhythms of God. It is in the everyday and
the commonplace that we learn patience,
acceptance, and contentment.

RICHARD J. FOSTER

O Lord, you have examined
my heart and know everything
about me.... You both precede and
follow me, and place your hand of
blessing on my head.

PSALM 139:1,5 TLB

March 1

March 2

God walks with us.... He scoops us
up in His arms or simply sits with us
in silent strength until we cannot avoid
the awesome recognition that yes,
even now, He is here.

GLORIA GAITHER

$\mathcal{T}$here is no mode of life
in the world more pleasing and
more full of delight than
continual conversation with God.

BROTHER LAWRENCE

March 3

March 4

*E*very moment is full of
wonder and God is always present.

Yet I am always with you;
you hold me by my right hand.

PSALM 73:23 NIV

*G*od's real love becomes
more than a covering cloak.
It saturates our every cell.

ROSE GOBLE

March 5

March 6

The Lord is good, a refuge
in times of trouble. He cares for
those who trust in him.

NAHUM 1:7 NIV

*R*ight now a moment
of time is fleeting by!
Capture its reality....
Become that moment.

PAUL CÉZANNE

March 7

March 8

One of the most wonderful things
about knowing God is that there's
always so much more to know,
so much more to discover.
Just when we least expect it,
He intrudes into our neat and tidy notions
about who He is and how He works.

JONI EARECKSON TADA

$\mathcal{G}$od's friendship is the
unexpected joy we find when we
reach His outstretched hand.

JANET L. WEAVER SMITH

March 9

March 10

From the world we see, hear,
and touch, we behold inspired visions
that reveal God's glory. In the sun's light,
we catch warm rays of grace and glimpse
His eternal design. In the birds' song, we hear
His voice and it reawakens our need of Him.
At the wind's touch, we feel His Spirit and
sense our eternal existence.

*T*he God who made the world and
everything in it is the Lord of heaven and earth
and does not live in temples built by hands.
And he is not served by human hands, as if he
needed anything, because he himself gives all
men life and breath and everything else.... God
did this so that men would seek him and perhaps
reach out for him and find him, though he is
not far from each one of us.

ACTS 17:24–27 NIV

March 11

March 12

If each moment is sacred—a time
and place where we encounter
God—life itself is sacred.

JEAN M. BLOMQUIST

$\mathcal{M}$ost new discoveries
are suddenly-seen things that
were always there.

SUSAN K. LANGER

MARCH 13

March 14

There is a unique kind of transparence about things and events. The world is seen through, and no veil can conceal God completely. So the pious man is ever alert to see behind the appearance of things a trace of the divine, and thus his attitude toward life is one of expectant reverence.

ABRAHAM JOSHUA HESCHEL

$\mathcal{B}$efore me, even as behind,
God is, and all is well.

JOHN GREENLEAF WHITTIER

March 15

March 16

The fulfillment of God's promise
depends entirely on trusting God
and his way, and then simply
embracing him and what he does.
God's promise arrives as pure gift.

ROMANS 4:16 THE MESSAGE

$\mathcal{S}$ometimes our light goes out
but is blown into flame by another
human being. Each of us owes
deepest thanks to those who have
rekindled this light.

ALBERT SCHWEITZER

March 17

Mᴀʀᴄʜ 18

Aꜱ a countenance is made
beautiful by the soul's shining through it,
so the world is beautiful by the
shining through it of God.

Fʀɪᴇᴅʀɪᴄʜ Hᴇɪɴʀɪᴄʜ Jᴀᴄᴏʙɪ

The "air" which our souls need also
envelops all of us at all times and on all sides.
God is round about us...on every hand,
with many–sided and all–sufficient grace.
All we need to do is to open our hearts.

OLE HALLESBY

March 19

March 20

Life...gives you the chance
to love and to work and to play
and to look up at the stars.

HENRY VAN DYKE

$\mathcal{M}$ay the Lord bless and
protect you; may the Lord's face radiate
with joy because of you; may he be
gracious to you, show you his favor,
and give you his peace.

NUMBERS 6:24–26 TLB

March 21

March 22

All the world is an
utterance of the Almighty.
Its countless beauties, its exquisite
adaptations, all speak to you of Him.

PHILLIPS BROOKS

*G*race and life.

Forgiveness of sin.

The defeat of death.

This is the hope Jesus gives.

This is the hope we need.

MAX LUCADO

March 23

March 24

*B*eauty is not
caused. It is.

EMILY DICKINSON

He has made everything
beautiful in its time.

ECCLESIASTES 3:11 NIV

*G*od is to be seen in the
light of a cottage window as well
as in the sun or the stars.

ARTHUR G. CLUTTON-BROCK

March 25

March 26

*S*atisfy us in the morning
with your unfailing love,
that we may sing for joy and
be glad all our days.

PSALM 90:14 NIV

*O*ur Lord has written the
promise of the resurrection,
not in books alone, but in every
leaf in springtime.

MARTIN LUTHER

March 27

March 28

God wants nothing from us
except our needs, and these furnish Him
with room to display His bounty when
He supplies them freely.... Not what I have,
but what I do not have, is the first point
of contact between my soul and God.

CHARLES H. SPURGEON

$\mathcal{S}$olitude liberates us from entanglements by carving out a space from which we can see ourselves and our situation before the Audience of One. Solitude provides the private place where we can take our bearings and so make God our North Star.

OS GUINNESS

MARCH 29

March 30

In comparison with this big world,
the human heart is only a small thing.
Though the world is so large, it is utterly
unable to satisfy this tiny heart.
Our ever growing soul and its capacities
can be satisfied only in the infinite God.
As water is restless until it reaches its level,
so the soul has no peace until it rests in God.

SADHU SUNDAR SINGH

*T*he steadfast love of the
Lord never ceases, his mercies
never come to an end; they are new
every morning; great is
your faithfulness.

LAMENTATIONS 3:22–23 NRSV

March 31

April 1

When we give the
Word of God space to live in our heart,
the Spirit of God will use it to
take root, penetrating the earthiest
recesses of our lives.

KEN GIRE

$\mathcal{G}$od who is goodness and truth is also beauty. It is the innate human and divine longing, found in the company of goodness and truth, that is able to recognize and leap up at beauty and rejoice and know that all is beautiful, that there is not one speck of beauty under the sun that does not mirror back the beauty of God.

ROBERTA BONDI

April 2

April 3

Our greatness rests solely
on the fact that God in His incomprehensible
goodness has bestowed His love upon us.
God does not love us because we are
so valuable; we are valuable because
God loves us.

HELMUT THIELICKE

*N*ature is the living,
visible garment of God.

GOETHE

April 4

April 5

Open your mouth and taste,
open your eyes and see—how good
God is. Blessed are you who run to him.
Worship God if you want the best;
worship opens doors to all his goodness.

PSALM 34:8–9 THE MESSAGE

*G*od wrote His loveliest poem on the day
He made the first silver poplar tree,
And set it high upon a pale-gold hill
For all the new enchanted earth to see.

GRACE NOLL

APRIL 6

April 7

God is everywhere and yet invisible,
silent, seemingly absent and indifferent....
We need more than a watchmaker who
winds up the universe and lets it tick.
We need love and mercy and forgiveness
and grace—qualities only a personal
God can offer.

PHILIP YANCEY

$\mathcal{G}$od wears Himself out through
the infinite thickness of time and space
in order to reach the soul and to captivate it....
The soul, starting from the opposite end,
makes the same journey that God made
towards it. And that is the cross.

SIMONE WEIL

APRIL 8

April 9

*T*his is and has been the Father's
work from the beginning—to bring us
into the home of His heart.

GEORGE MACDONALD

*T*he basic reality of God is plain enough.
Open your eyes and there it is!
By taking a long and thoughtful look at what
God has created, people have always been able
to see what their eyes as such can't see:
eternal power, for instance, and the
mystery of his divine being.

ROMANS 1:19–20 THE MESSAGE

April 10

April 11

Those who contemplate the beauty of the earth find reserves of strength that will endure as long as life lasts. There is symbolic as well as actual beauty in the migration of the birds, the ebb and flow of the tides, the folded bud ready for the spring. There is something infinitely healing in the repeated refrains of nature—the assurance that dawn comes after night, and spring after the winter.

RACHEL CARSON

$\mathcal{G}$od loves us for ourselves.
He values our love more than He
values galaxies of new created worlds.

A. W. TOZER

APRIL 12

April 13

As prayer moves into the subconscious mind, breathed longings of wonder and adoration seem always underneath and in the background of everything—a little like a tune that we suddenly realize we have been humming all day long.

RICHARD J. FOSTER

$\mathcal{I}$n all ranks of life the
human heart yearns for the beautiful;
and the beautiful things that
God makes are His gift to all alike.

HARRIET BEECHER STOWE

APRIL 14

April 15

The Lord is slow to anger
and great in power.... His way is in
the whirlwind and the storm,
and clouds are the dust of his feet.

NAHUM 1:3 NIV

*S*pring is God thinking in gold,
laughing in blue, and speaking in green.

FRANK JOHNSON

APRIL 16

April 17

All the things in this world
are gifts and signs of God's love
to us. The whole world is a
love letter from God.

PETER KREEFT

God knows the rhythm of my
spirit and knows my heart thoughts.
He is as close as breathing.

April 18

April 19

Forbid that I should walk through Thy beautiful world with unseeing eyes: Forbid that the lure of the market–place should ever entirely steal my heart away from the love of the open acres and the green trees: Forbid that under the low roof of workshop or office or study I should ever forget Thy great overarching sky.

JOHN BAILLIE

*W*hat marvelous love
the Father has extended to us!
Just look at it—we're called
children of God!

1 JOHN 3:1 THE MESSAGE

APRIL 20

April 21

*I*n God's wisdom, He frequently
chooses to meet our needs by
showing His love toward us through
the hands and hearts of others.

JACK HAYFORD

$\mathcal{W}$e don't walk spiritually by
electric light, but by a hand-held lantern.
And a lantern shows only the next
step—not several steps ahead.

AMY CARMICHAEL

APRIL 22

April 23

Where God is,
there is heaven–heaven!
Where His Majesty
reigns in glory.

TERESA OF AVILA

*T*he deep woods reveal God's presence.
The way the golden sunlight streaks through the
lush greens and browns of a summer wood is
nothing short of divine. In the fall the profusion
of colors makes every leaf a prayer. Winter's
snow transforms the woods into a cathedral.
Even the dark, drab hues of the woods in early
spring speak of hope and resurrection. It is a
place where I can be on a spiritual retreat.

RAYMOND K. PETRUCCI

April 24

April 25

My Presence will go
with you, and I will
give you rest.

EXODUS 33:14 NIV

You have not been sprinkled
with forgiveness. You have not been
spattered with grace. You have not been
dusted with kindness. You have been immersed
in it. You are submerged in mercy.
You are a minnow in the ocean of
his mercy. Let it change you!

MAX LUCADO

April 26

April 27

Our Creator would never
have made such lovely days, and given
us the deep hearts to enjoy them,
above and beyond all thought,
unless we were meant to be immortal.

NATHANIEL HAWTHORNE

$\mathcal{T}$his is my Father's world;

He shines in all that's fair.

In the rustling grass I hear Him pass;

He speaks to me everywhere.

MALTBIE D. BABCOCK

April 28

April 29

*G*od loves you in the
morning sun and the evening rain,
without caution or regret.

BRENNAN MANNING

$\mathcal{G}$od is able to make all grace
abound to you, so that in all things
at all times, having all that you need,
you will abound in every good work.

2 CORINTHIANS 9:8 NIV

April 30

May 1

$\mathcal{G}$o outside, to the fields, enjoy nature
and the sunshine, go out and try to recapture
happiness in yourself and in God.
Think of all the beauty that's still left in
and around you and be happy!

ANNE FRANK

*T*he very possibility of
friendship with God transfigures life.
This conviction...tends inevitably to
deepen every human friendship, to make
it vastly more significant.

HENRY CHURCHILL KING

May 2

May 3

For in the true nature of things,
if we will rightly consider, every green
tree is far more glorious than if it
were made of gold and silver.

MARTIN LUTHER

$\mathcal{T}$here is no limit to God's love.
It is without measure and its depth
cannot be sounded.

MOTHER TERESA

May 4

M ay 5

Seek the Lord your God, and you
will find Him if you seek Him with all
your heart and with all your soul.

DEUTERONOMY 4:29 NIV

*I*f we are children of God,
we have a tremendous treasure in nature
and will realize that it is holy and sacred.
We will see God reaching out to us in every
wind that blows, every sunrise and sunset,
every cloud in the sky, every flower that
blooms, and every leaf that fades.

OSWALD CHAMBERS

May 6

May 7

Isn't it a wonderful morning?
The world looks like something God had
just imagined for His own pleasure.

LUCY MAUD MONTGOMERY

The blossom cannot tell
what becomes of its fragrance as it
drifts away, just as no person can tell
what becomes of their influence
as they continue through life.

May 8

May 9

Grace and gratitude belong
together like heaven and earth.
Grace evokes gratitude like the
voice an echo. Gratitude follows grace
as thunder follows lightning.

KARL BARTH

$\mathcal{G}$od's love is meteoric,

his loyalty astronomic,

His purpose titanic,

his verdicts oceanic.

Yet in his largeness

nothing gets lost.

PSALM 36:5–6 THE MESSAGE

May 10

May 11

A rainbow stretches from
one end of the sky to the other.
Each shade of color, each facet of
light displays the radiant spectrum of God's
love—a promise that He will always
love each one of us at our worst
and at our best.

$\mathcal{T}$he Lord has done great things
for us, and we are filled with joy.

PSALM 126:3 NIV

May 12

May 13

God sends the brilliant light
of a rainbow to remind
us of His presence.

VERDELL DAVIS

$\mathcal{F}$or God is, indeed, a wonderful
Father who longs to pour out His mercy
upon us, and whose majesty is so
great that He can transform us
from deep within.

TERESA OF AVILA

May 14

May 15

*S*urely goodness and love
will follow me all the days of my
life, and I will dwell in the
house of the Lord forever.

PSALM 23:6 NIV

$\mathcal{W}$e may run, walk, stumble, drive, or fly, but let us never lose sight of the reason for the journey, or miss a chance to see a rainbow on the way.

GLORIA GAITHER

May 16

May 17

God is not an elusive dream
or a phantom to chase, but a divine
person to know. He does not avoid us,
but seeks us. When we seek Him,
the contact is instantaneous.

NEVA COYLE

$\mathcal{W}$here others see but the
dawn coming over the hill,
I see the soul of God
shouting for joy.

WILLIAM BLAKE

May 18

May 19

We need never shout across
the spaces to an absent God.
He is nearer than our own soul,
closer than our most secret thoughts.

A. W. TOZER

$\mathcal{L}$et the beloved of the Lord
rest secure in him, for he shields
him all day long, and the one the Lord
loves rests between his shoulders.

DEUTERONOMY 33:12 NIV

MAY 20

May 21

All the absurd little meetings,
decisions, and skirmishes that go to
make up our days. It all adds up to very little,
and yet it all adds up to very much. Our days
are full of nonsense, and yet not, because
it is precisely into the nonsense of our
days that God speaks to us words of
great significance.

FREDERICK BUECHNER

$\mathcal{I}$'ll tell you how
the sun rose—one ribbon at a time.

EMILY DICKINSON

Because of the tender mercy
of our God,...by which the rising
sun will come to us from heaven.

LUKE 1:78 NIV

May 22

May 23

God is the sunshine that
warms us, the rain that melts
the frost and waters the young plants.
The presence of God is a climate of
strong and bracing love, always there.

JOAN ARNOLD

*G*od has a wonderful plan for
each person He has chosen. He knew
even before He created this world
what beauty He would bring forth
from our lives.

LOUIS B. WYLY

May 24

May 25

For God is sheer beauty,

all–generous in love,

loyal always and ever.

PSALM 100:5 THE MESSAGE

*L*istening to God is a
firsthand experience.... God invites
you to vacation in His splendor.
He invites you to feel the touch of His hand.
He invited you to feast at His table.
He wants to spend time with you.

MAX LUCADO

May 26

May 27

In order that we finite beings
may apprehend God, He translates
His glory into multiple forms—into stars,
woods, waters, beasts, and the
bodies of men.

C. S. LEWIS

*T*he universe is orderly, and God
does not present us with confusion
but with clarity. The nature of God's
universe and God's character are, thus,
closely related. This world is as it
is at least in part because
God is who He is.

JAMES W. SIRE

May 28

May 29

Aware of our inbuilt resistance to grace, Jesus talked about it often. He described a world suffused with God's grace: where the sun shines on people good and bad; where birds gather seed gratis, neither plowing nor harvesting to earn them; where untended wildflowers burst into bloom on the rocky hillsides.

PHILIP YANCEY

The Lord will guide you always;
he will satisfy your needs
in a sun-scorched land.... You will be
like a well-watered garden, like a spring
whose waters never fail.

ISAIAH 58:11 NIV

May 30

May 31

God's love is like a river springing
up in the Divine Substance and flowing
endlessly through His creation,
filling all things with life and
goodness and strength.

THOMAS MERTON

*K*now by the light of faith
that God is present, and be content
with directing all your
actions toward Him.

BROTHER LAWRENCE

J u n e 1

June 2

Of the heavenly things God has
shown me, I can speak but a little word,
no more than a honeybee can carry
away on its foot from an overflowing jar.

MECHTILD OF MAGDEBURG

*O the depth of the riches and wisdom
and knowledge of God!*

ROMANS 11:33 NRSV

*G*od is with us in the midst
of our daily, routine lives. In the middle
of cleaning the house or driving somewhere
in the pickup.... Often it's in the middle of the
most mundane task that He lets us know He
is there with us. We realize, then, that there
can be no "ordinary" moments for people
who live their lives with Jesus.

MICHAEL CARD

June 3

June 4

You have made known
to me the path of life;
you will fill me with joy
in your presence, with eternal
pleasures at your right hand.

PSALM 16:11 NIV

*L*isten, be still and wait,
You'll hear all kinds of things:
A moth up on the windowpane,
Whir of wild birds on the wing.
Listen, be still and hear
The language of the wildflowers.
Be serene and patient; wait
For new sounds every hour.

MAMIE OZBURN ODUM

J u n e 5

June 6

The Infinite has sowed His name
in the heaven in burning stars,
but on the earth He has sowed
His name in tender flowers.

JEAN PAUL RICHTER

$\mathcal{G}$od loves to look at us, and loves
it when we will look back at Him.
Even when we try to run away from
our troubles...God will find us, bless us,
even when we feel most alone, unsure....
God will find a way to let us know that
He is with us in this place,
wherever we are.

KATHLEEN NORRIS

June 7

June 8

*T*he awe that we sense or
ought to sense when standing in the
presence of a human being is a moment
of intuition for the likeness of God
which is concealed in His essence.

ABRAHAM JOSHUA HESCHEL

*G*od made my life complete
when I placed all the pieces before him.
When I got my act together,
he gave me a fresh start....
God rewrote the text of my life
when I opened the book
of my heart to his eyes.

PSALM 18:20,24 THE MESSAGE

June 9

June 10

Who has seen the wind?
Neither you nor I;
But when the trees bow
down their heads,
The wind is passing by.

CHRISTINA ROSSETTI

A renewed mind has an
utterly changed conception, not only
of reality, but of possibility....
Impossibilities become possibilities.

ELISABETH ELLIOT

With man this is impossible,
but not with God; all things are
possible with God.

MARK 10:27 NIV

J u n e 11

June 12

To see a World in a Grain of Sand
And a Heaven in a Wild Flower,
Hold infinity in the palm of your hand
and Eternity in an hour.

WILLIAM BLAKE

$\mathcal{G}$od's heart is the most
sensitive and tender of all.
No act goes unnoticed, no matter
how insignificant or small.

RICHARD J. FOSTER

June 13

June 14

You answer us with awesome deeds of righteousness, O God our Savior, the hope of all the ends of the earth and of the farthest seas, who stilled...the roaring of their waves, and the turmoil of the nations. Those living far away fear your wonders; where morning dawns and evening fades you call forth songs of joy.

PSALM 65:5–8 NIV

$\mathscr{T}$he beauty of the earth,
the beauty of the sky, the order of the stars,
the sun, the moon, their very loveliness
is their confession of God.

AUGUSTINE

June 15

June 16

The best reason to pray is
that God is really there. In praying, our
unbelief gradually starts to melt. God moves
smack into the middle of even an ordinary day....
Prayer is a matter of keeping at it....
Thunderclaps and lightning flashes are very
unlikely. It is well to start small and quietly.

EMILIE GRIFFIN

$\mathcal{L}$et us believe that God
is in all our simple deeds and
learn to find Him there.

A. W. TOZER

June 17

June 18

Sunset

The day is done,

The sun has set,

Yet light still tints the sky;

My heart stands still

In reverence,

For God is passing by.

RUTH ALLA WAGER

I call on you, O God, for you
will answer me; give ear to me and
hear my prayer. Show the wonder of your
great love.... Keep me as the apple of your eye;
hide me in the shadow of your wings.

PSALM 17:6–8 NIV

June 19

June 20

That is God's call to us—simply to
be people who are content to live
close to Him and to renew the kind
of life in which the closeness is
felt and experienced.

THOMAS MERTON

$\mathcal{T}$he God who holds the whole world in His hands wraps Himself in the splendor of the sun's light and walks among the clouds.

J u n e 21

J u n e 22

God looks at the world through
the eyes of love. If we, therefore,
as human beings made in the image
of God also want to see reality rationally,
that is, as it truly is, then we, too, must
learn to look at what we see with love.

ROBERTA BONDI

$\mathcal{G}$race is no stationary thing,
it is ever becoming. It is flowing straight
out of God's heart. Grace does nothing but
reform and convey God. Grace makes
the soul conformable to the will of God.
God, the ground of the soul, and
grace go together.

MEISTER ECKHART

J u n e 23

June 24

God's peace...is far more
wonderful than the human mind
can understand. His peace will keep
your thoughts and your hearts
quiet and at rest.

PHILIPPIANS 4:7 TLB

*I*t is God's will that we believe
that we see Him continually, though it
seems to us that the sight be only partial; and
through this belief He makes us always to gain
more grace, for God wishes to be seen, and He
wishes to be sought, and He wishes to be
expected, and He wishes to be trusted.

JULIAN OF NORWICH

June 25

June 30

*B*e sure to remember that
nothing in your daily life is so
insignificant and so inconsequential that
God will not help you by
answering your prayer.

OLE HALLESBY

$\mathcal{M}$ay our lives be illumined
by the steady radiance
renewed daily,
of a wonder,
the source of which
is beyond reason.

DAG HAMMARSKJÖLD

July 1

July 2

Anything that exists in any
way must necessarily have
its origin in God.

THOMAS AQUINAS

*I*n the forest we can rise
above our worldly care;
In the forest we may find
tranquility and share
The silence and the secret strength
of great and ancient trees—
Sturdy oaks and silver birches,
laughing in the breeze.

PATIENCE STRONG

July 3

July 4

When you draw close to God,
God will draw close to you.

JAMES 4:8 TLB

We must drink deeply from
the very Source the deep calm and
peace of interior quietude and refreshment
of God, allowing the pure water of divine
grace to flow plentifully and unceasingly
from the Source itself.

MOTHER TERESA

July 5

July 6

We can go through all the
activities of our days in joyful awareness
of God's presence with whispered prayers
of praise and adoration flowing
continuously from our hearts.

RICHARD J. FOSTER

*H*e doesn't come in the
roaring thunder, as we expect.
He doesn't write in blazing lightning as
it flashes across the clouds, even though we
watch for Him there. His voice won't be in
the rushing wind or in the pounding
rhythm of the waves breaking against the
seashore. He simply comes to us
in a still small voice.

July 7

July 8

There is nothing but God's grace.
We walk upon it; we breathe it; we live
and die by it; it makes the nails and
axles of the universe.

ROBERT LOUIS STEVENSON

$\mathcal{G}$od is our refuge and strength,
an ever-present help in trouble.
Therefore we will not fear, though the
earth give way and the mountains fall into
the heart of the sea, though its waters roar
and foam and the mountains quake with their
surging.... Be still, and know that I am God;
I will be exalted among the nations,
I will be exalted in the earth.

PSALM 46:1–3,10 NIV

July 9

July 10

God comes to us before
we go to Him.... This is God's habit.
God came to Abraham when there
was nothing to come to, just an old man
at a dead end. But that's God for you.
That's the way God likes to work.
He comes to old men and to infants,
to sinners and to losers. That's grace.

JAMES VAN THOLEN

$\mathcal{T}$here is a native, elemental
homing instinct in our souls which
turns us to God as naturally as the
flower turns to the sun.

RUFUS M. JON

July 11

July 12

*G*od still draws near to me in
the ordinary, commonplace, everyday
experiences and places.... He comes in
surprising ways.

HENRY GARIEPY

$\mathcal{G}$od cares for the world He created, from the rising of a nation to the falling of the sparrow. Everything in the world lies under the watchful gaze of His providential eyes, from the numbering of the days of our life to the numbering of the hairs on our head. When we look at the world from that perspective, it produces within us a response of reverence.

KEN GIRE

July 13

July 14

You're all I want in heaven!
You're all I want on earth!...
I'm in the very presence of
God—oh, how refreshing it is!

PSALM 73:25,28 THE MESSAGE

*I*t is an extraordinary and beautiful
thing that God, in creation...works with
the beauty of matter; the reality of things;
the discoveries of the senses, all five of them;
so that we, in turn, may hear the grass growing;
see a face springing to life in love and laughter....
The offerings of creation...our glimpses of truth.

MADELEINE L'ENGLE

July 15

July 16

We both believe, and disbelieve a
hundred times an Hour,
which keeps Believing nimble.

EMILY DICKINSON

I do believe; help me
overcome my unbelief!

MARK 9:24 NIV

*I*f God is present at every point
in space, if we cannot go where He is not,
cannot even conceive of a place where He is not,
why then has not that Presence become the one
unanswerably celebrated fact of the world?...
People do not know if God is here. What a
difference it would make if they knew.

A. W. TOZER

July 17

July 18

A living, loving God can and
does make His presence felt, can and
does speak to us in the silence of our hearts,
can and does warm and caress us till
we no longer doubt that He is near,
that He is here.

BRENNAN MANNING

$\mathcal{A}$s the deer pants for
streams of water, so my soul pants
for you, O God. My soul thirsts for
God, for the living God.

PSALM 42:1–2 NIV

July 19

July 20

Because God created the
Natural—invented it out of His love
and artistry—it demands our reverence.

C. S. Lewis

*L*ook at the stars. The most universally awesome experience that mankind knows is to stand alone on a clear night and look at the stars. It was God who first set the stars in space; He is their Maker and Master—they are all in His hands and subject to His will. Such are His power and His majesty. Behold your God!

J. I. PACKER

July 21

July 22

I often think flowers are the angels' alphabet whereby they write on hills and fields mysterious and beautiful lessons for us to feel and learn.

LOUISA MAY ALCOTT

*W*hen we pray, we immerse
ourselves in the living
presence of God.

EUGENE PETERSON

July 23

July 24

For the soul of every living thing
is in the hand of God, and the
breath of all mankind.

JOB 12:10 TLB

The goodness of God is
infinitely more wonderful than we
will ever be able to comprehend.

A. W. TOZER

July 25

July 26

$\mathcal{G}$od's nature is given me.
His love is jealous for my life.
All His attributes are woven into
the pattern of my spirit. What a God is this!
His life implanted in every child.
Thank you, Father, for this.

JIM ELLIOT

$\mathcal{T}$o love conditionally is against
God's nature. Just as it's against your
nature to eat trees and against mine to
grow wings, it's against God's nature
to remember forgiven sins.

MAX LUCADO

July 27

July 28

When God finds a soul that
rests in Him and is not easily moved,
He operates within it in His own manner.
That soul allows God to do great things within
it. He gives to such a soul the key to the
treasures He has prepared for it so that it
might enjoy them. And to this same soul
He gives the joy of His presence which
entirely absorbs such a soul.

CATHERINE OF GENOA

*F*or all God's words are right,
and everything he does is worthy of
our trust. He loves whatever is just and good;
the earth is filled with his tender love. He merely
spoke, and the heavens were formed, and
all the galaxies of stars. He made the oceans,
pouring them into his vast reservoirs.

PSALM 33:4–7 TLB

July 29

July 30

Evening after evening in
the summer, I have gone to see the
white clover fall asleep in the meadow....
Everywhere in the dusk the white
clover leaves are sleeping in an
attitude of worship.

MARY WEBB

*L*et us give all that lies within us...to pure praise, to pure loving adoration, and to worship from a grateful heart—a heart that is trained to look up.

AMY CARMICHAEL

July 31

A u g u s t 1

*L*ife is not intended to be simply
a round of work, no matter how interesting
and important that work may be. A moment's
pause to watch the glory of a sunrise or
a sunset is soul satisfying, while a bird's
song will set the steps to music all day long.

LAURA INGALLS WILDER

*H*e is everything that is
good and comfortable for us. He is our
clothing that for love wraps us, clasps us,
and all surrounds us for tender love.

JULIAN OF NORWICH

A u g u s t 2

August 3

May the Lord continually
bless you with heaven's blessings
as well as with human joys.

PSALM 128:5 TLB

$\mathcal{W}$e can look to God as
our Father. We can have a personal
sense of His love for us and His
interest in us, for He is concerned
about us as a father is concerned
for his children.

BILLY GRAHAM

A u g u s t 4

Aᴜɢᴜsᴛ 5

𝒯he love of the Father is like
a sudden rain shower that will pour
forth when you least expect it, catching
you up into wonder and praise.

RICHARD J. FOSTER

$\mathcal{L}$isten to your life. See it for the fathomless mystery that it is. In the boredom and pain of it no less than in the excitement and gladness: touch, taste, smell your way to the holy and hidden heart of it because in the last analysis all moments are key moments and life itself is grace.

FREDERICK BUECHNER

August 6

August 7

The daisy was glad to stand
out in the grass...it felt very grateful;
and when the sun went down it folded
its leaves and went to sleep, and
dreamed all night about the sun.

HANS CHRISTIAN ANDERSEN

*M*y frame was not hidden from
you when I was made in the secret place.
When I was woven together in the depths of
the earth, your eyes saw my unformed body.
All the days ordained for me
were written in your book
before one of them came to be.

PSALM 139:15–16 NIV

August 8

August 9

Do we not dwell in the gallery of our God? Isn't the sky His canvas and humanity His magnum opus? Are we not encircled by artistry? Sunsets burning. Waves billowing. And isn't the soul His studio? The birthing of love, the bequeathing of grace. All around us miracles pop like fireflies—souls are touched, hearts are changed.

Max Lucado

$\mathcal{T}$he sunshine dancing on
the water, the lulling sound of waves rolling
into the shore, the glittering stars against the
night sky—all God's light, His warmth, His
majesty—our Father of light reaching
out to us, drawing each of us
closer to Himself.

AUGUST 10

August 11

The call of God is the call to be human, to embrace our humanity in all of its ambiguity.... The call of God is a summons to embark upon a journey of faith whose destiny is not always apparent.

RANDALL BALMER

The huge dome of the sky is of
all things sensuously perceived the most like
infinity. When God made space and worlds that
move in space, and clothed our world with air,
and gave us such eyes and such imaginations as
those we have, He knew what the sky would
mean to us.... We cannot be certain that this
was not indeed one of the chief purposes
for which Nature was created.

C. S. LEWIS

August 12

August 13

The Lord who created you says...
I have called you by name; you are mine.
When you go through deep waters
and great trouble, I will be with you.

ISAIAH 43:1–2 TLB

*W*orship is transcendent wonder.

THOMAS CARLYLE

AUGUST 14

August 15

Drop Thy still dews of quietness,
 Till all our strivings cease;
Take from our souls the strain and stress,
 And let our ordered lives confess
 The beauty of Thy peace.

JOHN GREENLEAF WHITTIER

*T*he heart...is the human spirit,
and the only thing in us that God will
accept as the basis of our relationship to Him.
It is the spiritual plane of our natural existence,
the place of truth before God, from where
alone our whole lives can become eternal.

DALLAS WILLARD

AUGUST 16

August 17

Someone said to me once
that we can see the features of
God in a single smile. Look for that
smile in the people you meet.

CHRISTOPHER DE VINCK

*Y*ou, O God, are both tender
and kind, not easily angered,
immense in love,
and you never, never quit.

AUGUST 18

August 19

*G*od's touch...lights the
world with color and renews
our hearts with life.

JANET L. WEAVER SMITH

*L*ife is meant to be lived from a Center,
a divine Center...a Life who speaks in us and
through us to the world. We have all heard this
holy Whisper at times.... But too many of us
have heeded the Voice only at times.... We have
not counted this Holy Thing within us to be
the most precious thing in the world.

THOMAS R. KELLY

A u g u s t 20

August 21

The wind rushing through
the grass, the thrush in the treetops,
and children tumbling in senseless
mirth stir in us a bright faith in life.

DONALD CULROSS PEATTIE

*T*he place where God calls you to
is the place where your deep
gladness and the world's
deep hunger meet.

FREDERICK BUECHNER

AUGUST 22

August 23

I call on you, O God,
for you will answer me; give ear
to me and hear my prayer.
Show the wonder of your great love....
Keep me as the apple of your eye;
hide me in the shadow of your wings.

PSALM 17:6–8 NIV

Woven in a perfect way,
a blanket of stars covers the night sky,
each star set in its place, reflecting its perfect
light. All the stars together make a grand
display, glimmering and shimmering in
a unique expression of praise to the
Creator of them all.

August 24

August 25

You, O God, are the Lord of the mountains and the valleys. As I travel over mountains and through valleys, I am beneath Your feet. You surround me with every kind of creature.... Open my eyes to see their beauty, that I may perceive them as the work of Your hands. In Your power, in Your thought, all things are abundant.

ROBERT VAN DE WEYER

$\mathcal{G}$od is here! I hear His voice
While thrushes make the woods rejoice.
I touch His robe each time I place
My hand against a pansy's face.
I breathe His breath if I but pass
Verbenas trailing through the grass.
God is here! From every tree
His leafy fingers beckon me.

MADELEINE AARON

August 26

August 27

This voice that calls to us out of the everyday moments of life is called the wisdom of God. This wisdom is infused into nature and the laws that govern her, and into human nature and the laws that govern it.

KEN GIRE

The Lord is gracious and merciful,
slow to anger and abounding in steadfast love.
The Lord is good to all, and his compassion
is over all that he has made.... The Lord is
faithful in all his words, and
gracious in all his deeds.

PSALM 145:8–9,13 NRSV

August 28

August 29

All that is good, all that is true,
all that is beautiful, all that is beneficent,
be it great or small, be it perfect or fragmentary,
natural as well as supernatural, moral as
well as material, comes from God.

JOHN HENRY NEWMAN

*W*ithout the Way, There is no going;
Without the Truth, There is no knowing;
Without the Life, There is no living.

THOMAS À KEMPIS

Jesus answered, "I am the way and
the truth and the life. No one comes to
the Father except through me."

JOHN 14:6 NIV

A u g u s t 30

A u g u s t 31

Every one of us as human
beings is known and loved by the
Creator apart from every other
human on earth.

JAMES DOBSON

$\mathcal{I}$f God is here for us and not
elsewhere, then in fact this place is
holy and this moment is sacred.

ISABEL ANDERS

September 1

September 2

We throw open the doors to
God and discover at the same moment that he
has already thrown open his door to us.
We find ourselves standing where we always
hoped we might stand out in the wide open
spaces of God's grace and glory.

ROMANS 5:2 THE MESSAGE

$\mathcal{A}$lways be in a state of
expectancy, and see that you leave
room for God to come in as He likes.

OSWALD CHAMBERS

S e p t e m b e r 3

September 4

Beauty born of beauty breeds
beauty in every way.... A person who
is given words of beauty is a person who
will express beauty.... All beauty can
be traced, ultimately, to God.

CHRISTOPHER DE VINCK

$\mathcal{D}$on't ever let yourself get so
busy that you miss those little but important
extras in life—the beauty of a day...the smile of a
friend...the serenity of a quiet moment alone.
For it is often life's smallest pleasures and
gentlest joys that make the biggest and
most lasting difference.

September 5

September 6

The remarkable truth is that
our choices matter, not just to us
and our own destiny but, amazingly,
to God Himself and the
universe He rules.

PHILIP YANCEY

*Y*ou give them drink from
your river of delights. For with you
is the fountain of life; in your
light we see light.

PSALM 36:8 NIV

S e p t e m b e r 7

September 8

The mystery of life is that the Lord of life cannot be known except in and through the act of living. Without the concrete and specific involvements of daily life we cannot come to know the loving presence of Him who holds us in the palm of His hand.... Therefore, we are called each day to present to our Lord the whole of our lives.

HENRI J. M. NOUWEN

*N*ot knowing when the dawn
will come I open every door.

EMILY DICKINSON

S eptember 9

September 10

Prayer makes your heart
bigger, until it is capable of
containing the gift of God Himself.

MOTHER TERESA

$\mathcal{G}$od's love never ceases. Never....
Our faith does not earn it anymore than our
stupidity jeopardizes it. God doesn't love
us less if we fail or more if we succeed.
God's love never ceases.

MAX LUCADO

September 11

September 12

Your thoughts—how rare,
how beautiful! God, I'll never comprehend
them! I couldn't even begin to count
them—any more than I could count the
sand of the sea. Oh, let me rise in the
morning and live always with you!

PSALM 139:17–18 THE MESSAGE

*B*efore anything else, above all else,
beyond everything else, God loves us.
God loves us extravagantly, ridiculously,
without limit or condition.
God is in love with us...God yearns for us.

ROBERTA BONDI

September 13

September 14

If it can be verified, we don't need faith.... Faith is for that which lies on the other side of reason. Faith is what makes life bearable, with all its tragedies and ambiguities and sudden, startling joys.

MADELEINE L'ENGLE

*S*avor little glimpses of God's
goodness and His majesty, thankful for
the gift of them: winding pathways through
the woods, a bright green canopy overhead,
and dappled sunshine falling all around,
warm upon our faces.

September 15

September 16

Dear Lord, grant me the grace
of wonder. Surprise me, amaze me,
awe me in every crevice of your universe....
Each day enrapture me with your
marvelous things without number.
I do not ask to see the reason for it all;
I ask only to share the wonder of it all.

ABRAHAM JOSHUA HESCHEL

*H*e is not far from each one of us.

For in him we live and move

and have our being.

ACTS 17:27–28 NIV

September 17

September 18

We encounter God in the ordinariness of life, not in the search for spiritual highs and extraordinary, mystical experiences, but in our simple presence in life.

BRENNAN MANNING

$\mathcal{N}$othing taken for granted;
everything received with gratitude;
everything passed on with grace.

G. K. CHESTERTON

September 19

September 20

All things are created by God and therefore good. All that is desirable in things is an image of the supremely desirable God.... There is simply nothing else to desire except God or God's images and reflections.... All the different things we desire are really one; for they are reflections of aspects of God.

PETER KREEFT

*G*od waits for us in the inner
sanctuary of the soul.
He welcomes us there.

RICHARD J. FOSTER

September 21

September 22

*N*o eye has seen, nor ear
heard, nor the human heart conceived,
what God has prepared for those
who love him.

1 CORINTHIANS 2:9 NRSV

*L*ook deep within yourself and
recognize what brings life and grace
into your heart. It is this that can be
shared with those around you.

You are loved by God.

This is an inspiration to love.

CHRISTOPHER DE VINCK

S e p t e m b e r 23

September 24

It's simple things, like a glowing sunset, the sound of a running stream or the fresh smell in a meadow that cause us to pause and marvel at the wonder of life, to contemplate its meaning and significance. Who can hold an autumn leaf in their hand, or sift the warm white sand on the beach, and not wonder at the Creator of it all?

$\mathcal{T}$he fruit of our placing all things
in His hands is the presence of His
abiding peace in our hearts.

HANNAH WHITALL SMITH

September 25

September 26

*G*od is the friend of silence.
Trees, flowers, grass grow in silence.
See the stars, moon, and sun how
they move in silence.

MOTHER TERESA

Our God gives you everything you need,
makes you everything you're to be.

2 THESSALONIANS 1:2 ABRAHAM

September 27

September 28

*T*he patterns of our days are
always changing...rearranging...and each
design for living is unique...graced
with its own special beauty.

God moves in a mysterious way
His wonders to perform;
He plants His footsteps in the sea,
And rides upon the storm.

WILLIAM COWPER

September 29

September 30

The world is charged
with the grandeur of God.

GERARD MANLEY HOPKINS

$\mathcal{T}$he great thing to remember
is that, though our feelings come and go,
God's love for us does not.

C. S. LEWIS

October 1

October 2

Can you fathom the mysteries of God?
Can you probe the limits of the Almighty?
They are higher than the heavens—what can
you do? They are deeper than the depths of
the grave—what can you know?
Their measure is longer than the
earth and wider than the sea.

JOB 11:7–9 NIV

$\mathcal{T}$he moment you begin to
delight in beauty, your heart
and mind are raised.

BASIL HUME

October 3

October 4

To pray is to change.
This is a great grace. How good of
God to provide a path whereby our lives
can be taken over by love and joy and peace
and patience and kindness and goodness
and faithfulness and gentleness
and self-control.

RICHARD J. FOSTER

I still find each day too short
for all the thoughts I want to think,
all the walks I want to take, all the
books I want to read, and all the friends
I want to see. The longer I live, the
more my mind dwells upon the beauty
and the wonder of the world.

JOHN BURROUGHS

O c t o b e r 5

October 6

Sunshine spills through
autumn-colored leaves, lighting up
their brilliance like stained-glass windows
in a great cathedral, expressing the wonder
of God's love, declaring His glory.

$\mathcal{G}$od promises to love me
all day, sing songs all through the
night! My life is God's prayer.

PSALM 42:8 THE MESSAGE

October 7

October 8

The rare and beautiful experiences
of divine revelation are moments of special gifts.
Each of us, however, lives each day with special
gifts which are a part of our very being, and life
is a process of discovering and developing these
God-given gifts within each one of us.

$\mathcal{T}$his is the real gift: we have been given the breath of life, designed with a unique, one-of-a-kind soul that exists forever—whether we live it as burden or a joy or with indifference doesn't change the fact that we've been given the gift of being now and forever. Priceless in value, we are handcrafted by God, who has a personal design and plan for each of us.

October 9

October 12

There is far more to your inner
life than the food you put in your stomach,
more to your outer appearance than the clothes
you hang on your body. Look at the ravens,
free and unfettered, not tied down to a job
description, carefree in the care of God.
And you count far more.

LUKE 12:22–23 THE MESSAGE

$\mathcal{W}$e come this morning—
Like empty pitchers to a full fountain,
With no merits of our own,
O Lord—open up a window of heaven,
And lean out far over the battlements of glory,
And listen this morning.

JAMES WELDON JOHNSON

October 13

October 14

If we are children of God, we have
a tremendous treasure in nature and will
realize that it is holy and sacred. We will see
God reaching out to us in every wind that
blows, every sunrise and sunset, every
cloud in the sky, every flower that blooms,
and ever leaf that fades.

OSWALD CHAMBERS

*O*nce we discover how to
appreciate the timeless values in our
daily experiences, we can enjoy
the best things in life.

HARRY HEPNER

October 15

October 16

Grace is something you can never get but can only be given. There's no way to earn it or deserve it or bring it about any more than you can deserve the taste of raspberries and cream or earn good looks.... A good night sleep is grace and so are good dreams. Most tears are grace. The smell of rain is grace. Somebody loving you is grace.

FREDERICK BUECHNER

*G*od is light, pure light;
there's not a trace
of darkness in him.

1 JOHN 1:5 THE MESSAGE

October 17

October 18

And I have felt
A presence that disturbs me with the joy
Of elevated thoughts; a sense sublime
Of something far more deeply interfused,
Whose dwelling is the light of setting suns.

WILLIAM WORDSWORTH

$\mathcal{A}$t the sound of a child's pure laugh or the sight of a father holding his baby for the first time, incredible joy pushes upward, spilling over. Our hearts were made for joy. Our hearts were made to enjoy the One who created them. Too deeply planted to be much affected by the ups and downs of life, this joy is a knowing and a being known by our Creator. He sets our hearts alight with radiant joy.

October 19

October 20

It is in silence that the soul
most accepts God.

*In quietness and trust
is your strength.*

ISAIAH 30:15 NIV

$\mathcal{C}$alm me, O Lord, as you stilled the storm,

Still me, O Lord, keep me from harm.

Let all the tumult within me cease,

Enfold me, Lord, in your peace.

CELTIC TRADITIONAL

October 21

October 22

The voice of the Lord is over
the waters; the God of glory thunders,
the Lord thunders over the mighty waters.
The voice of the Lord is powerful; the
voice of the Lord is majestic.

PSALM 29:3-4 NIV

$\mathcal{L}$et God have you, and let
God love you—and don't be surprised
if your heart begins to hear music you've
never heard and your feet learn to
dance as never before.

MAX LUCADO

October 23

October 24

*S*pread love everywhere you go:
first of all in your own home.
Give love to your children, to a wife
or husband, to a next-door neighbor.

Mother Teresa

*N*othing in all creation is so
like God as stillness.

MEISTER ECKHART

Be sill, and know that I am God;
I will be exalted among the nations.

PSALM 46:10 NIV

October 25

October 26

The God of the universe—the One who created everything and holds it all in His hand—created each of us in His image, to bear His likeness, His imprint. It is only when Christ dwells within our hearts, radiating the pure light of His love through our humanity that we discover who we are and what we were intended to be. There is no other joy that reaches as deep or as wide or as high—there is no other joy that is more complete.

$\mathcal{W}$ith the Lord a day is like a thousand
years, and a thousand years are like a day.
The Lord is not slow in keeping his promise,
as some understand slowness.

He is patient with you.

2 PETER 3:8–9 NIV

October 27

October 28

*L*ove has its source in God,
for love is the very essence of His being.

KAY ARTHUR

*H*ave confidence in God's mercy,
for when you think He is a long way
from you, He is often quite near.

THOMAS À KEMPIS

October 29

October 30

The best things are nearest:
breath in your nostrils, light in your eyes,
flowers at your feet, duties at your hand,
the path of God just before you.

ROBERT LOUIS STEVENSON

$\mathscr{T}$he things that matter the most
in this world, they can never
be held in our hand.

GLORIA GAITHER

October 31

November 1

I'm asking God for one thing,
only one thing: To live with him in
his house my whole life long.
I'll contemplate his beauty;
I'll study at his feet. That's the only quiet,
secure place in a noisy world.

PSALM 27:4–5 THE MESSAGE

$\mathcal{A}$nything that exists
in any way must necessarily
have its origin in God.

THOMAS AQUINAS

November 2

November 3

Infinite and yet personal,
personal and yet infinite, God may
be trusted because He is the True One.
He is true, He acts truly, and He speaks truly....
God's truthfulness is therefore
foundational for His trustworthiness.

OS GUINNESS

*P*rayer is such an ordinary,
everyday, mundane thing.
Certainly, people who pray are no
more saints than the rest of us. Rather, they
are people who want to share a life with
God, to love and be loved, to speak and
to listen, to work and to be at rest in
the presence of God.

ROBERTA BONDI

November 4

November 5

You are a creation of God
unequaled anywhere in the universe....
Thank Him for yourself and then for
all the rest of His glorious handiwork.

NORMAN VINCENT PEALE

The Lord longs to be gracious to you;

He rises to show you compassion.

For the Lord is a God of justice.

Blessed are all who wait for Him!

ISAIAH 30:18 NIV

November 6

November 7

Today is a new day. You will get out of it just what you put into it. If you have made mistakes, even serious mistakes, there is always another chance for you.... You may have a fresh start any moment you choose, for this thing that we call "failure" is not the falling down, but the staying down.

MARY PICKFORD

$\mathcal{I}$t is in silence that
God is known, and through
mysteries that He
declares Himself.

ROBERT H. BENSON

November 8

November 9

We are made to reach out
beyond our grasp.

OSWALD CHAMBERS

*Let us know, let us press on to know
the Lord; his going forth is sure as the dawn;
he will come to us as the showers, as the
spring rains that water the earth.*

HOSEA 6:3 RSV

The beauty of the sunbeam
lies partly in the fact that God does not
keep it; He gives it away to us all.

DAVID SWING

November 10

November 11

The deeper your love,
the higher it goes; every cloud is a flag
to your faithfulness. Soar high in the
skies, O God! Cover the whole earth
with your glory!

PSALM 57:10-11 THE MESSAGE

*A*t times it is only necessary
to rest one's self in silence for a few
minutes, in order to take off the pressure
and become wonderfully refreshed.

DRESSER

November 12

November 13

Joy is the touch of God's finger. The object of our longing is not the touch but the Toucher. This is true of all good things—they are all God's touch. Whatever we desire, we are really desiring God.

PETER KREEFT

*T*here is plenitude in God....
God is a vast reservoir of blessing
who supplies us abundantly.

<small>EUGENE PETERSON</small>

November 14

November 15

When I need a dose of wonder
I wait for a clear night and go look for the
stars.... In the country the great river of the
Milky Way streams across the sky, and I
know that our planet is a small part of that
river of stars.... Often the wonder of the
stars is enough to return me to
God's loving grace.

MADELEINE L'ENGLE

$\mathcal{Y}$our heavenly Father knows
your needs. He will always give
you all you need from day to day.

LUKE 12:30–31 TLB

November 16

November 17

I believe that life is given so we
may grow in love, and I believe that
God is in me as the sun is in the color
and fragrance of a flower—the Light in my
Darkness, the Voice in my Silence.

HELEN KELLER

$\mathcal{I}$ would maintain that thanks
are the highest form of thought,
and that gratitude is happiness
doubled by wonder.

G. K. CHESTERTON

November 18

November 19

The universe is but one
vast symbol of God.

THOMAS CARLYLE

Gratitude...is not something
we do at all. Rather, it is a medium
of grace, a gift of God that softens the
heart and enables it to see and hear
and receive the things that
come to it from God.

ROBERTA BONDI

November 20

November 21

Where can I go from your Spirit?
Where can I flee from your presence?
If I go up to the heavens, you are there;
if I make my bed in the depths, you are there.
If I rise on the wings of the dawn, if I settle
on the far side of the sea, even there your
hand will guide me, your right hand
will hold me fast.

PSALM 139:7–10 NIV

*I*n extravagance of soul we seek
His face. In generosity of heart, we glean His
gentle touch. In excessiveness of spirit,
we love Him and His love comes
back to us a hundredfold.

RHODES TRICIA MCCARY

November 22

November 23

If you keep this comparison always in mind—that of a castle with a wondrous throne within—God may use it to draw you into His presence, where He bestows the favors that He loves to grant.

TERESA OF AVILA

*G*ratitude. More aware of what
you have than what you don't. Recognizing
the treasure in the simple—a child's hug,
fertile soil, a golden sunset. Relishing in the
comfort of the common—a warm bed,
a hot meal, a clean shirt.

MAX LUCADO

November 24

November 25

There is not a heart but has its
moments of longing, yearning for
something better, nobler, holier
than it knows now.

HENRY WARD BEECHER

*W*hat a wonderful God
we have—he is...the source of
every mercy, and the one who so
wonderfully comforts and strengthens us.

2 CORINTHIANS 1:3–4 TLB

November 26

November 27

We are made for God,
and nothing less will
really satisfy us.

BRENNAN MANNING

*T*he wonder of our Lord is that
He is so accessible to us in the common things
of our lives: the cup of water...breaking of the
bread...welcoming children into our arms...
fellowship over a meal...giving thanks. A
simple attitude of caring, listening, and
lovingly telling the truth.

NANCIE CARMICHAEL

November 28

December 1

To you, O Lord, I lift up my soul;
in you I trust, O my God.... Show me
your ways, O Lord, teach me your paths;
guide me in your truth and teach me, for
you are God my Savior and my
hope is in you all day long.

PSALM 25:1,4–5 NIV

$\mathcal{L}$ife in the presence of God
should be known to us in conscious
experience. It is a life to be enjoyed
every moment of every day.

A. W. Tozer

December 2

December 3

*God is within all things,
but not included; outside all things,
but not excluded, above all things,
but not beyond their reach.*

POPE GREGORY I

$\mathscr{P}$rayer is the human response
to the perpetual outpouring of love
by which God lays siege to every soul.
When our reply to God is most direct
of all, it is called adoration. Adoration is
spontaneous yearning of the heart to worship,
honor, magnify, and bless God.

RICHARD J. FOSTER

December 4

December 5

*A*ll the way to heaven is
heaven begun to the one who walks
near enough to God to hear the
secrets He has to impart.

E. M. BOUNDS

$\mathscr{F}$or God Himself works in
our souls, in their deepest depths,
taking increasing control as we are
progressively willing to be prepared
for His wonder.

THOMAS R. KELLY

December 6

December 7

The Lord is the great God,
the great King above all gods.
In his hand are the depths of the earth,
and the mountain peaks belong to him.
The sea is his, for he made it, and
his hands formed the dry land.

PSALM 95:3–5 NIV

$\mathcal{T}$o seek God means first of all
to let yourself be found by Him.

December 8

December 9

$\mathcal{Y}$ou can revive your sense of wonder by merely saying to yourself: Suppose this were the only time. Suppose this sunset, this moonrise, this symphony, this buttered toast, this sleeping child, this flag against the sky...suppose you would never experience these things again! Few things are commonplace in themselves.

ARTHUR GORDON

$\mathcal{G}$od's fingers can touch nothing
but to mold it into loveliness.

GEORGE MACDONALD

December 10

December 11

Nothing we can do will make the Father love us less; nothing we do can make Him love us more. He loves us unconditionally with an everlasting love. All He asks of us is that we respond to Him with the free will that He has given to us.

NANCIE CARMICHAEL

*U*ntil I am essentially united
with God, I can never have full
rest or real happiness.

JULIAN OF NORWICH

December 12

December 13

God gets down on His knees
among us; gets on our level and shares
Himself with us. He does not reside
afar off and send diplomatic messages,
He kneels among us.... God shares
Himself generously and graciously.

EUGENE PETERSON

$\mathcal{E}$very good and perfect gift
is from above, coming down
from the Father of the heavenly
lights, who does not change
like shifting shadows.

JAMES 1:17 NIV

December 14

December 15

$\mathcal{A}$ quiet morning with a loving
God puts the events of the upcoming
day into proper perspective.

JANETTE OKE

*W*e desire many things,
and God offers us only one thing.
He can offer us only one thing—Himself.
He has nothing else to give.
There is nothing else to give.

PETER KREEFT

December 16

December 17

We are celebrating the feast
of the Eternal Birth which God the
Father has borne and never ceases
to bear in all eternity.... But if it takes
not place in me, what avails it?
Everything lies in this,
that it should take place in me.

MEISTER ECKHART

$\mathcal{G}$od loves us; not because we are
lovable but because He is love,
not because He needs to receive
but because He delights to give.

C. S. LEWIS

December 18

December 19

"The virgin will be with child
and will give birth to a son, and they
will call him Immanuel"—which means,
"God with us."

MATTHEW 1:23 NIV

*I*ncarnation, breath becoming
speech through teeth and tongue, spirit
becoming word, silence becoming prayer,
the holy dream becoming
the holy face.

FREDERICK BUECHNER

December 20

December 21

But God's own descent into flesh was meant
As a demonstration that the supreme merit
Lay in risking spirit in substantiation....
Spirit enters flesh and for all it's worth
Charges into earth in birth after birth
Ever fresh and fresh.

ROBERT FROST

$\mathcal{G}$od bless you and utterly
satisfy your heart...with Himself.

AMY CARMICHAEL

December 22

December 23

Christmas hath a beauty
Lovelier than the world can show:
For Christmas bringeth Jesus,
Brought for us so low.
Earth, strike up your music,
Birds that sing and bells that ring;
Heaven hath answering music
For all Angels soon to sing.

CHRISTINA ROSSETTI

*F*or to us a child is born, to us
a son is given, and the government
will be on his shoulders.
And he will be called Wonderful
Counselor, Mighty God, Everlasting
Father, Prince of Peace.

ISAIAH 9:6 NIV

December 24

December 25

Creator of heaven and earth,
He was born on earth under heaven.
Unspeakably wise,
He is wisely speechless.
Filling the world,
He lies in a manger...
He is both great in the nature of God,
and small in the form of a servant.

AUGUSTINE

$\mathcal{T}$he most vivid memories of
Christmases past are usually not of gifts
given or received, but of the spirit of love,
the special warmth of Christmas worship,
the cherished little habits of the home,
the results of others acting
in the spirit of Christ.

LOIS RAND

December 26

December 27

To the children of God there stands,
behind all that changes and can change,
only one unchangeable joy. That is God.

HANNAH WHITALL SMITH

*S*o how do I act as if You're alive?
How do the cells of my body, the same ones
that sweat and urinate and get depressed and toss
and turn in bed at night—how do these cells
carry around the splendor of the God of the
universe in a way that leaks out for others
to notice? How do I love even one person
with the love You came to bring?

PHILIP YANCEY

December 28

December 29

Thanks be to God for
his indescribable gift!

2 CORINTHIANS 9:15 NIV

*A*bove all give me grace to use
these beauties of earth without me and
this eager stirring of life within me as a
means whereby my soul may rise
from creature to Creator, and
from nature to nature's God.

JOHN BAILLIE

December 30

December 31

*Y*ou do not know what you are going to do; the only thing you know is that God knows what He is doing.... It is this attitude that keeps you in perpetual wonder—you do not know what God is going to do next.

OSWALD CHAMBERS

5 M 5 - Pitman's colleg
 - short hand
died - Mld Magdela
need help with cond
Letter writting

- Robert - H;Imam's
horse breeder -
Parents concern - H I
'no one will ever as
you - mixed marrie
- H I - 10 yrs. of happine
when baiBachi die
- angry H I - I am
by your side alw

BESTSELLING
IN THE

Dear Reader,

It's time to shine the spotlight on six special authors—bestsellers you wouldn't want to miss!

We've selected stories by some of your favorite authors to give you a chance to meet old friends or discover new ones. These novelists are strong, prolific women who write the stories that you've told us you love, and each is distinguished by a unique style and an uncanny ability to touch the heartstrings of her readers.

If you're not acquainted with the work of Alicia Scott, Sherryl Woods, Barbara Boswell, Kristine Rolofson, Janice Kay Johnson and Muriel Jensen, now's your big chance! And if you are, you may want to have a peek at page six for a more complete listing of books by the author of this volume.

Take a chance on a sure thing, and enjoy all six of our Bestselling Authors in the Spotlight!

The Editors

Praise for
SHERRYL WOODS

"Ms. Woods mixes delicious touches of humor
and charming characters into simply
delightful reading."
—*Romantic Times*

"Ms. Woods once again demonstrates her gift
for creating provocative characters
and weaves her special brand of humor
throughout the story."
—*Rendezvous*

SHERRYL WOODS

JOSHUA
AND THE
COWGIRL

Silhouette Books

Published by Silhouette Books

America's Publisher of Contemporary Romance

SILHOUETTE BOOKS

JOSHUA AND THE COWGIRL

Copyright © 1991 by Sherryl Woods

Copyright © 1998 by Sherryl Woods

ISBN 0-373-48373-2

Dear Reader,

When I first wrote *Joshua and the Cowgirl,* it was as much of a Western adventure for me as it was for Joshua. Like this Southern-bred accountant, I am a product of milder, less harsh climates. Then, after growing up in Virginia and spending ten years in Ohio, I discovered it was possible to be warm in February. I moved to Florida, and there was no turning back.

Well, almost no turning back. I'm now splitting my year between Key Biscayne, an island suburb of Miami, and Colonial Beach, Virginia, the town where I spent summers as a child. I'm sure you can guess which months are spent where.

In addition to liking warmth and hating snow almost as much as Joshua, I was also as unfamiliar with ranching as he was when he first arrived in Wyoming. But I was fascinated with the Western myths, and especially those sexy Western heroes. In the years since, I have set many of my books on ranches, including the multibook AND BABY MAKES THREE miniseries about those wonderful, strong-willed Adams men and women in Los Pinos, Texas.

I hope you enjoy going back to this first Western adventure as much as I enjoyed writing it and discovering a whole new world for the romantic heroes I love to create.

All good wishes,

Sherryl Woods

Books by Sherryl Woods

Silhouette Special Edition

Safe Harbor #425
Never Let Go #446
Edge of Forever #484
In Too Deep #522
Miss Liz's Passion #573
Tea and Destiny #595
My Dearest Cal #669
Joshua and the Cowgirl #713
*Love #769
*Honor #775
*Cherish #781
*Kate's Vow #823
*A Daring Vow #855
*A Vow To Love #885
The Parson's Waiting #907
One Step Away #927
Riley's Sleeping Beauty #961
†Finally a Bride #987
‡A Christmas Blessing #1001
‡Natural Born Daddy #1007
‡The Cowboy and His Baby #1009
*‡The Rancher and His
  Unexpected Daughter* #1016
**A Ranch for Sara #1083
**Ashley's Rebel #1087
**Danielle's Daddy Factor #1094
††The Littlest Angel #1142
††Natural Born Trouble #1156

Silhouette Desire

Not at Eight, Darling #309
Yesterday's Love #329
Come Fly with Me #345
A Gift of Love #375
Can't Say No #431
Heartland #472
One Touch of Moondust #521
Next Time... Forever #601
Fever Pitch #620
Dream Mender #708

Silhouette Books

Silhouette Summer Sizzlers 1990
"A Bridge to Dreams"

* Vows
† Always a Bridesmaid!
‡ And Baby Makes Three
** The Bridal Path
†† And Baby Makes Three:
  The Next Generation

Please address questions and book requests to:
Silhouette Reader Service
U.S.: 3010 Walden Ave., P.O. Box 1325, Buffalo, NY 14269
Canadian: P.O. Box 609, Fort Erie, Ont. L2A 5X3

Chapter One

When he stepped out of his car, placed his three-hundred-dollar Italian loafers into a foot of fresh snow and found himself face-to-face with an inquisitive cow, Joshua knew deep in his gut that Wyoming was not going to be one bit better this time around. The sophisticated world of international financial consultant Joshua Ames did not include cows. At the globe-trotting pace he lived, it didn't even include tame little kittens or rambunctious puppies.

Admittedly his life had taken a certain predictable turn these last few years, but he found comfort in that. He lived in a world of fast sports cars, like the flashy red convertible he'd rented at the airport in Cheyenne before he'd realized that Indian summer was not a concept with which Wyoming weather was acquainted. With so much of his life spent in five-star hotels, he felt settled only in the luxury of exclusive skyscrapers—like the oceanfront tower he'd reluctantly left behind in Florida or the cozy pied-à-terre he kept that overlooked Central Park in New York. Joshua's life, even on the rare occasions when he bothered with breakfast, even included thick cream for his fresh raspberries. However, in all of his thirty-seven eventful years his world had never, ever included a face-to-face encounter with the source of that cream.

Until now.

The creature had ambled close enough that he could feel its hot breath. Images of the pageantry and violence of the bullrings in Spain flashed through his mind with untimely clarity. His own breath caught in his throat. Good Lord, surely this was a gentle milk cow, *not* a bull! He nervously checked for some sign of ferocity and impending threat in its limpid brown eyes, but saw only vague curiosity. He wasn't about to get intimate enough to investigate for more positive identification of its gender.

Joshua took a cautious step backward, butted into a strand of barbed wire, yelped and muttered a string of colorful obscenities, most of them directed at his client and best friend, Cal Rivers. Scratch that. *Former best friend.* Joshua was never going to forgive him for this or any of his other myriad sins, which seemed to be stacking up like old newspapers now that marriage had turned Cal's previously razor-sharp brain to lovesick mush.

Retaliation held a certain rapidly growing appeal. Maybe he'd just bungle Cal's corporate books so thoroughly that an entire team of accountants working around the clock wouldn't be able to untangle them by tax time. Maybe he'd help him choose a few highly questionable junk bonds for his steadfastly risk-free portfolio. Maybe he'd triple his usual fees and take that long-delayed vacation in Paris at Cal's expense.

Or maybe he'd just shoot him. Yeah, that was it, Joshua decided with enthusiasm. There had to be a shotgun someplace on this godforsaken ranch. He would load it and then track down his former best friend. When he found Cal, he'd blow him to smithereens for dragging him away from civilization for the second time in the year and a half since Cal had been reunited with his family. To think that he had actually encouraged the reconciliation! Joshua should have known better. He should have realized that sooner or later a happily settled Cal would insist that he come back to this place that reminded him all too vividly of a time in his life he'd spent years trying to forget.

Not that Joshua hadn't tried to protect himself from such an eventuality. Joshua had warned Cal way back then that he would not ever set foot on this desolate ranch again. He had sworn to die first. He was not interested in dust. He did not appreciate wide open spaces. The sunsets in Florida were quite enough, not that he paid much attention to them. Joshua had clients far less intractable than Mrs. Caroline Whitfield McDonald, Cal's maternal grandmother. He was not a bookkeeper, which was what Mrs. McDonald sorely needed. Those were all good reasons, solid, self-protective reasons.

Joshua had rarely admitted, even to himself, that the real reasons went much deeper. Behind the excuses were the memories. Dredged up from the depths of the past, the memories recalled the scared, overprotected boy he had once been; a boy who had been thoroughly, painfully out of his element in a rough-and-tumble environment much like this.

Now that he was standing up to his ankles in snow, he realized he should have mentioned that, as well. Snow was meant for ski slopes in winter. There wasn't a mountain in sight in this empty, dreary part of Wyoming. To top it off, it was barely September. He'd left ninety-degree temperatures back home. He shivered in the harsh, blustery air and wondered if he'd be taking his life in his hands to try maneuvering around the cow to reach the jacket in the car. Since it was only a suit jacket, he decided it wasn't worth it. He'd still be freezing his butt off.

Okay. Cal had made a mistake in not mentioning the snow. But Joshua was sure he had stated emphatically that he absolutely, positively was not interested in getting up close and personal with livestock unless he was betting a financial bundle on cattle futures.

Cal, damn him, had laughed at each and every protest. Hooted, in fact. He'd bided his time, then lured

Joshua out here by reminding him of their years of friendship, their long business association. He'd thrown in a healthy suggestion of desperation. Right now, with that cow staring him in the face, Joshua knew all about desperation. As far as he could tell, Wyoming was fraught with it.

"I see you've met Jezebel," a husky feminine voice, threaded with all-too-familiar gloating laughter, said just when he was contemplating the precise details of murder and mayhem. Desperation took a new twist as his thoughts veered dramatically and predictably.

Garrett. Traci Maureen Garrett, to be precise—and Joshua was the kind of man who insisted on being precise. Working with numbers—huge numbers—required it. Surviving around Garrett, he'd discovered, also demanded a similar degree of attentiveness.

Traci Maureen Garrett had very nearly driven him nuts when they'd met nearly a year and a half ago. Her smug attitude, sharp tongue and sly humor had stung. If the slam-bang, ready-for-combat pace of his heartbeat right this second was any indication, she was going to do it again. He considered it yet another black mark against Cal. A mere eighteen months ago he had been a serene, contented man. Now he was one inch from another jab of barbed wire, six inches from a fire-breathing cow and laughing distance from a know-it-all female who was obviously delighting in his fix.

Above all, though, Joshua Ames was a proud man. No cow—or cowgirl—was going to see even the faintest hint that he was intimidated. He mustered his most confident smile and turned slowly, never letting that creature out of his line of vision.

"Jezebel?" he said. "Is there much room for wickedness in the bovine world?"

"Let's just say that Jezebel always manages to find trouble."

A fascinating, dimpled smile, that also meant trouble, met his gaze. That never forgotten, daring, tempting smile kept him from lingering too long on the thick braid of sunlight-blond hair, blue velvet eyes and long—endlessly long—slender legs encased in snug denim. Not trendy denim, he noticed with a faint sigh of regret, but faded, hard-working jeans meant to withstand life on a cattle ranch.

His gaze settled on her smile, the curve of generous lips, and stayed there—reluctantly. The punch-in-the-belly impact of that smile hadn't diminished one bit. Unfortunately. It had been yet another reason to steer as far away from this ranch as possible. Traci Maureen Garrett, who had a spark of sheer mischief in her eyes, was *not* the woman of his dreams. *She* couldn't be. Surely God wouldn't be cruel enough to let him fall for a woman who managed a cattle ranch!

"I see," he said, adopting what he hoped was suitable nonchalance for a man who felt as if he'd been pole-axed for the second time in his life. The first time had been a year and a half earlier. The unlikely, impossible Garrett had figured heavily in both incidents.

"Is she a family pet?" he inquired.

"Nope. Actually she's about one step away from

being sent to market. My personal hunch is that she knows it and is trying to ingratiate herself around the house.''

The concept of this cow being someone's dinner appealed to Joshua in a perverse way that told him a lot about his overall mood with regards to this latest assignment. From the indulgent expression in Garrett's eyes, however, he decided he'd best keep his bloodthirsty opinion to himself. She was obviously fond of this cow, which made her contradictory willingness to send it off to slaughter a little chilling.

That was part of what troubled him about Garrett. One minute he was totally and completely enthralled by her careless, untamed beauty and captivated by her quick mind. Then, in less time than it took to saddle a horse, he was reminded that she was tough as nails, and as uncompromising and mule-headed as one of those self-made millionaires with whom he occasionally had to tangle over financial policy. Maybe this time, if he could catch his breath around her, he'd be able to figure her out.

Maybe, if he was very, very lucky, he'd be able to get her out of his system. To his regret, all these months and the clever efforts of innumerable beautiful, sophisticated women hadn't accomplished it. Maybe proximity would...if it didn't get him into a hell of a lot of trouble first.

Garrett was not proud of herself. She knew she was enjoying Joshua Ames's discomfort a little too much.

A kind, generous woman would take pity on him and send the perfectly harmless Jezebel fleeing back to the pasture the cow had escaped from. Unfortunately some crazy quirk in her psyche kept her from feeling much pity for this city slicker who obviously felt so much disdain for her beloved world of blue skies and wide open spaces.

The man's attitude was the pits. Only her fondness for her boss, Mrs. Caroline Whitfield McDonald, had kept her from telling him exactly what she thought of him the last time he'd breezed in here with his slightly crooked nose poked in the air. Mrs. Mac, as she was known around the ranch, obviously needed him—or thought she did. It was Garrett's personal opinion that Mrs. Mac had run the ranch quite capably and successfully without interference from a know-it-all financial genius from the east. Her grandson, however, had thought otherwise. He'd appeared out of the blue, taken one look at the admittedly haphazardly kept books and sent for the cavalry. No doubt he feared for his inheritance. Garrett hadn't quite dared to suggest as much to Mrs. Mac.

"I'm surprised you came back," Garrett said, taking a no-trespassing stance that worked especially well on the cowboys around town.

"No more than I am," Joshua admitted with disarming candor.

"Why did you? Surely you have more important things to do than balance the accounts around here. Isn't your forte spending other people's money?"

"Actually, it's increasing their money," he said, amusement lurking in the depths of his eyes. There was no hint of false modesty, no suggestion that he ever dared to lose any of their cash.

"Since I doubt that Mrs. Mac lets you near her capital, why are you here?"

"Cal insisted."

"And everyone jumps to do his bidding, don't they?" Garrett couldn't keep the resentful note out of her voice.

"Friends do," Joshua said softly. "What's Cal asked you to do?"

"I don't take orders from him."

"I can imagine," he said, grinning suddenly. "I don't suppose that's kept Cal from giving them. Has he been throwing his weight around? Asking impertinent questions? Stepping on your managerial toes?"

She shrugged. "Cal can make all the suggestions he wants to Mrs. Mac. It's his ranch or will be soon enough."

Joshua's gaze narrowed. "And that really infuriates you, doesn't it? Were you hoping to get it for yourself?"

The too-close-to-the-mark dig irritated her. "Not the way you mean. I was hoping for a chance to buy into it," she said.

His features instantly softened with apparent understanding. The suggestion of pity only angered her.

"I'm sure Cal would work a deal with you," Joshua said. "I don't think he's interested in keeping the place for himself. Cal's got enough on his hands with that horse farm down in Florida. Now that he's won a couple of races, he's more convinced than ever that raising Thoroughbreds is the life for him.''

Joshua's aggrieved tone told her what he thought of that idea. If he'd meant to reassure her, though, he'd missed the mark. Cal's disinterest wouldn't help her situation a bit. Mrs. Mac had her mind set on giving this place to her grandson. Her legacy, she said. His birthright. She'd been trying her damnedest to manipulate him into accepting it. Knowing Mrs. Mac, sooner or later she'd have her way. Then, even if Cal were willing to sell someday, Garrett wasn't likely to have the kind of cash it would take to impress him.

"It'll be years before I can pay Cal what it's worth," she told Joshua honestly. "He'll probably sell it off long before that." She hoped Joshua Ames couldn't tell just how much that hurt. Garrett had been so darned close for the first time in her life to getting what she wanted, and now it was slipping away. It was all but certain the ranch was going to a man who didn't give a damn about it and was likely to sell it to strangers at the first opportunity.

"Maybe I could talk to him."

The offer sounded so sincere and was so totally unexpected that Garrett found herself staring at him in astonishment. "Why would you do that?"

"Beats me," Joshua said. "Maybe it's your charming personality."

Garrett flushed, taking the pointed barb square on

the chin. The man hadn't been here five minutes and she was taking out all of her anger and frustration on him. It wasn't Joshua's fault she was going to lose her dream. It wasn't even his fault that he was a greenhorn. She surveyed the thick blond hair, the stubborn chin, the wreck of a nose that ruined the perfection of his face but created interest. Everything about Joshua Ames shouted money and glamour, *except* that nose. It spoke of street-tough masculinity. She wondered who had dared to bloody it and under what circumstances. Then, perversely, Garrett wondered why she cared.

She was still wondering that when he said, "Do you suppose we could get inside before I freeze to death?"

Snug in the warmth of her sheepskin jacket, she couldn't resist taunting him. "It's mild out here. You should be here in January."

He shuddered visibly. "God forbid!"

Garrett grinned. "Go on in. Mrs. Mac's waiting for you."

"And Cal?"

"He's flown back to Florida," she said, enjoying the quick blaze of fury that swept into his eyes before he could discreetly mask it.

"He's gone where?" Joshua bellowed so loudly that Jezebel took flight and headed back to the pasture.

"Left just as the snow started. Should be landing back there about now," she confirmed cheerfully.

"I'm going to kill him."

"Seems to me you're going to have to catch up with him first."

He appeared torn between the desire to flee and resignation. "You don't have to enjoy this so damned much," he muttered.

"Why not? We get so little entertainment out here in the boondocks."

Joshua winced, but his guilt was apparently fleeting. Then a wicked, dangerous gleam filled his eyes. That glint, hot enough to melt snow, warmed her as no sheepskin jacket ever had. His gaze raked over her from head to toe. Very slowly. "Perhaps I can find other ways to change that."

Garrett's cheeks flamed at the deliberate taunt. She knew how to handle the straightforward passes thrown by hopeful cowboys. She was less sure how to deal with sly, flirtatious comments meant to rattle her. Garrett knew instinctively, though, that she couldn't allow Joshua to see that his seductive remark bothered her in the slightest. Poking her hands into her pockets, she looked him straight in the eye and declared with bold impudence, "I doubt you're man enough."

Instead of the stunned outrage she'd expected, the insult merely drew one of his devastating killer smiles. "I guess we'll just have to see about that, won't we?" Joshua challenged, running a finger along the line of her jaw. Deep inside her something responded to that deliberate touch, something that scared the daylights out of her.

"When hell freezes over!" she retorted, swiping his hand away and trying to ignore the spine-tingling effect of his low chuckle of amusement.

He glanced around meaningfully at the endless snow-covered vistas and smiled. A distressingly masculine expression of smug satisfaction spread slowly across his face, finally reaching his eyes. Those sexy, fascinating blue-green eyes, Garrett decided, were going to be her undoing. His gaze locked on hers and no matter how hard she willed it, she couldn't seem to tear her gaze away.

"Looks to me like it already has," he said, more laughter threading through his rich voice.

"Hmm?" she said blankly.

Joshua gestured at their surroundings. "Hell, sweetheart. Looks to me like it's already frozen over."

Chapter Two

Garrett blistered the blue skies with every epithet she could think of to describe Joshua's character and his heritage. She was still muttering under her breath when she charged into the barn at full throttle.

"Whoa," Red Grady said, catching her by the elbows and steadying her as she plowed into his solid, barrel chest. "Who lit a fire under you?"

"That man," she said, as if that would be explanation enough.

"At last check we had about a dozen men on the premises. Care to be more specific?" the ranch foreman inquired, barely containing a grin.

"Joshua Ames."

"Ah," Red murmured knowingly. "He does have a

way of getting under your skin. Why is that, do you suppose?"

"Because he is an obnoxious, know-it-all jerk." Garrett grabbed the saddle soap and went to work on her saddle. Red propped a booted foot on a sawhorse and watched her.

"If you rub much harder, you're going to wear out the leather," he observed finally. "Want me to beat the man up for you?"

Garrett's gaze shot up to meet his laughing eyes. "You'd do it, too, wouldn't you?" she said, more grateful than ever for Red's enduring friendship.

It had been nearly fourteen years since Red had found her waiting tables in that roadside diner halfway between Cheyenne and the ranch. He'd befriended her over eggs and grits and a stack of pancakes that still awed her. Garrett had been seven months pregnant, exhausted and lonely. An uncomplicated, caring man, Red had stood by her, listening to her fears and her dreams. A month before her daughter had been born, he'd brought her to meet Mrs. McDonald. The job interview had gone smoothly. She had known that Red had stuck his neck out for her and that, very likely, Mrs. McDonald had invented a job for her. He'd wanted to see her settled before the birth. She would never forget Red for that. Nor would she ever take advantage of him.

"I can handle Joshua Ames," she told him now, though she hadn't the faintest idea how.

He tucked a finger under her chin and tilted her head

up. "You know I'd do anything for you, though. That's a given. You need, you ask, okay?"

Garrett wrapped her hand around his larger, callused one and pressed it to her cheek. "Thanks, Red."

His cheeks turned a shade of red very nearly as bright as his curly, untamed hair. He backed off a step and shoved his hands into his pockets. "No need for thanks. As far as I'm concerned, you and your daughter, Casey, are family and families stick together." He grinned at her. "Besides, I wouldn't mind taking a punch at the competition on my own account anyway."

The offhanded remark was made cheerfully enough, but it troubled Garrett just the same. She knew Red was fond of her. In his own stumbling way he'd told her more than once that he'd be pleased to share a future with her. If she was ever going to trust a man, Red would be the one, but something had always held her back. Today, encountering Joshua again and feeling her blood race hot and wild at his slightest touch, she recognized what had kept her from that commitment to Red. Garrett didn't want the kind of danger Joshua represented, but settling for less wasn't in the cards for her, either. She'd rather go through life alone, accountable only to herself and to Casey. It was a choice she'd made years ago. Until the day she'd met Joshua Ames, she'd never questioned it.

That alone told her far too much about the threat he posed. With any luck, though, he would be gone in a day or two and she would survive this second attack on her senses unscathed. If there was even the most remote chance of it happening any other way, well, there was always Red's offer to punch the man out for her.

Joshua paced from one end of the cluttered parlor to the other, dodging musty, old-fashioned furniture and cursing Cal as he went. A fire blazed, which should have made the room welcoming. Instead the house felt stuffy and overheated, making it especially oppressive after the icy air outside and Garrett's equally chilly reception.

Joshua's temper, usually slow to rise, was leashed so tightly that the slightest irritation was likely to set him off. It was his experience that Mrs. McDonald could irritate the dickens out of him in less than ten seconds flat. He could hardly wait for her to waltz in here in that imperious way she had and try to explain why he was here and Cal was basking in the Florida sun. He heard the sharp tapping of her cane and prepared himself for a royal battle.

"Mr. Ames, it's so lovely to have you back with us again," she greeted him in a voice that rang with a strength belied by her slow, obviously painful approach. Joshua found himself moving swiftly to grasp her elbow as she eased herself onto a Victorian chair covered in faded brocade. Though the chair looked miserably uncomfortable, she sat in it regally. Her back was not quite as ramrod straight as he'd remembered, but her still coal-black hair was swept up in a crowning braid that added to the impression of stature and quiet dignity. He might have been fooled had he not seen her enter the room or looked closely at her face.

Filled with compassion, Joshua pulled up a chair and sat opposite her. He'd heard about her osteoporosis, but this was the first evidence he'd seen of its devastating effect. His anger died in the face of her valiant struggle to brave a pain that shadowed the snapping blue of her eyes and drained the color from her cheeks. The disease had clearly worsened since his last visit.

"Can I get you something?" he offered.

A faint smile tugged at the grim set of her mouth. "I can still manage to ring for the help, young man. Tea will be served shortly."

Joshua sat back, chastened yet amused. Obviously nothing had weakened her spirit. In that instant his reluctant respect for the gritty, eighty-two-year-old rancher grew tremendously. He vowed to do nothing more to undercut her bravery. This was one situation in which chivalry was most likely to be deemed pity and refused out of hand.

"Where's Cal?" he asked far more mildly than he'd intended.

Her mouth turned down. "Home, I expect. He said something about those infernal horses of his, then took off."

"Even though he knew I was coming?"

"I suspect his sudden hurry might have had something to do with my offer to build him his own place out here, so I could watch my great-grandbabies grow up."

Joshua grinned reluctantly. "That would do it."

"I don't know why the man's so stubborn," she grumbled. "It makes perfect sense for him to live out here. I know I could convince Marilou, if he'd just give me a little time to work on her. She likes the sense of family continuity here."

"And you're perfectly willing to use his wife's weakness for family ties to manipulate Cal. No wonder he's run for his life. I'd be surprised if he ever brings Marilou and the baby back again."

Mrs. McDonald scowled at him impatiently. "I might have known you'd stick up for him. Can't any of you see that this place will all be his one of these days? He needs to know how to run it."

"Cal certainly doesn't need it and he says he doesn't want it."

"Stubborn fool. He's ignoring reality. I am not about to change my will at this late date. If nothing else, he should think of his children."

"He can provide for his children well enough and I suspect he comes by the stubborn need to do so naturally."

The observation drew a nod of reluctant satisfaction. "I expect he does at that. I suppose I ought to count it as a blessing that he's not some namby-pamby sort I can push around."

"You certainly should," Joshua agreed, though less than ten minutes ago he'd been wanting to shove Cal around a little himself. "So, why am I here? Are you hoping I'll be more amenable to your whims?"

She chuckled. "That's not a label I'd pin on you, young man. You're worse than that grandson of mine. Cal insisted on dragging you out here, though. Took one look at the books and nearly went into cardiac arrest. He snuck off to call you right after that."

"I set up a very simple bookkeeping procedure for you the last time I was here. Didn't you use it?"

She waved a gnarled, bejeweled hand indifferently. "More or less."

Joshua groaned. "What about the accountant in Cheyenne I contacted for you? Why didn't you call him?"

Her chin rose. "I didn't like him."

"Why?"

"He was too young."

"He was nearly sixty."

"I didn't like that awful after-shave he used. Smelled all prissy to me. How can you trust a man who douses himself with scent like that?"

Joshua muttered an oath, forgetting that Mrs. McDonald's hearing was sharp as ever. She stiffened. "Young man, I do not tolerate language like that in my house."

"Sorry," he said automatically. "I don't suppose it crossed your mind that you're looking for excuses to keep Cal around and involved in things?"

She sniffed indignantly. "Well, of course I am." She sighed. "Not that it's doing me any good."

"How'd he convince you to let me come back?"

"He didn't ask."

"I could leave," he offered, possibly a shade too enthusiastically. She settled a sharp gaze on him and shook her head.

"You might as well stay, now that you're here. I've put you in the same room at the top of the stairs. If you need anything, just ask Elena. You should be comfortable enough there for the next few weeks."

An immediate knot formed in the pit of his stomach. "Weeks?" he repeated.

"According to Cal, that's how long it's likely to take to straighten out the mess we've made of things. Garrett tries, but she has too much to do around here as it is. We both sort of figured if there was money in the bank accounts at the end of the year we'd done okay."

Joshua listened to the casual tone and detected the false note at once. Mrs. McDonald had not survived all these years as a widow in this hard, unforgiving environment with an attitude like that. She'd probably counted every penny, then squeezed the last cent of value out of each and every one.

He met her gaze head on. "You're an old fraud, you know that?" he said.

Flustered by the direct challenge, she feigned a coughing fit, then finally shrugged and winked at him. "Maybe so. Maybe not. You'll know better once you've seen those books."

"I wouldn't put it past you to keep a duplicate set, all nice and tidy, locked away in your bedroom."

"What if I do? You won't find it."

"Maybe I will," he warned. "It'd mean a lot to me not to come here again."

"Enough to sneak in there and risk getting shot with the rifle I keep by my bed?"

Joshua thought of the danger Garrett represented to his equilibrium and those acres and acres of snow-covered land just crawling with cattle. "Could be," he told her. "I guess we'll both just have to wait and see."

"Por favor," Elena pleaded as Garrett edged anxiously toward the kitchen door. "The *señora* wishes you to dine with her and her guest tonight. The little *señorita*, as well."

"I promised Casey I'd make pizza tonight," Garrett improvised, a trifle desperately. She did not want to sit at that oversized dining-room table and make small talk with a man whose gaze heated her blood as Joshua's did. It had been incredibly disconcerting this afternoon to discover that she was not nearly as immune to men as she'd believed all these years. It was particularly distressing that it was Joshua Ames who'd awakened her senses from a fourteen-year slumber.

"I cannot tell the *señora* that," Elena said. A crafty note crept into the housekeeper's voice. "You will have to tell her," she said triumphantly.

"Tell me what?" Mrs. McDonald said just then, putting an end to the test of wills.

Garrett sighed. "I was just explaining to Elena that I'd promised Casey pizza tonight. I'm sorry. I won't be able to join you for dinner."

"Casey is already in the parlor entertaining Joshua."
Garrett's spirits sank. "Oh."

Mrs. McDonald nodded victoriously. "That's settled then. Hold dinner for a half hour, Elena. Mr. Ames and I will have a sherry in the parlor, while we wait for Garrett to change."

Garrett looked down at her dirt-smeared jeans and muddy boots. She was achingly tired. If Mrs. Mac was determined to drag her to this dinner, she could just take her as she was. For an instant she was childishly tempted to tell her just that. In the end, though, her fondness for Mrs. Mac, as well as a streak of determined pride, kept her from doing it. "I'll only be a minute," she promised wearily.

It was a full half hour before she reappeared, but judging from the approval in Joshua's eyes, her attempts to downplay her femininity had been wasted. His slow examination took in the bulky, shapeless blue sweater that fell below her hips, as if he were imagining every concealed curve. His gaze lingered appreciatively on the stretch pants below, then rose again to settle on her face. The only makeup she wore was a pale pink lipstick, but he seemed fascinated by it. Finally, as if he, too, felt disconcerted, he jerked his gaze away, moved toward the silver tray set on the desk and poured himself another glass of sherry from the crystal decanter. He drank it down in one gulp.

To Garrett's dismay Mrs. Mac's curious gaze was fixed on him the entire time. Garrett recognized at once the spark of interest that flared in her eyes at the scene before her. The old woman was an inveterate match-maker. She'd made Garrett's marital status her pet project years ago. Garrett's stubborn refusal to go along with any of her schemes had finally dimmed her hopes, but obviously the last few minutes had rekindled the old fervor.

"Hey, Mom," Casey said. "Mr. Ames said he'd teach me to play chess. Isn't that great?"

Garrett didn't like the idea of her daughter getting chummy with Joshua. It would be just one more reason why she'd have to be nice to him and at the moment she wanted to put up as many hostile barriers as possible. "Between your schoolwork and your chores, I don't know when you'll have time."

"Perhaps Casey could be excused from her chores while Joshua is here," Mrs. McDonald suggested with sly innocence.

"Absolutely not," Garrett protested.

Casey's face fell. "Oh, Mom, please. You know I've been wanting and wanting to learn. You don't know how and Mrs. Mac says he plays much better than she does. Besides, it won't be for long. I deserve a vacation. All the other hands get one."

Garrett grinned despite herself. She ruffled her thirteen-year-old's unruly golden curls. Casey prided herself on being one of the cowboys. Since she'd been old enough to sit in a saddle, the men had tolerantly allowed her along on their roundups, teaching her everything they knew about ranching and probably more than she needed to know about the world. It had made her precocious, but it had also given her a sense of responsibility. She handled more chores than most children her age and she did it without complaint.

"How long a vacation do you figure you deserve?" Garrett asked.

Casey turned adoring eyes on Joshua, who in turn was watching Garrett's reaction. "How long will you be here?" Casey asked him.

He hesitated as if waiting for guidance from one of the women. "Long enough to teach you what you need to know to beat Mrs. Mac," he promised finally.

"I can almost do that now," Casey scoffed.

"Then maybe you ought to save that vacation for something else," he said.

Casey shook her head adamantly. "No. It's my vacation. I get to choose what to do during my vacation. I really, really want to learn how to play chess."

"I suppose it won't hurt if you take a few days to hone your skills," Garrett conceded finally, unwilling to rob her daughter of a few hours of excitement and special attention. Besides, if Joshua was occupied at the chessboard, he'd have far less time to trouble her with his penetrating glances.

Mrs. Mac rose just then. "Shall we go into dinner, ladies? Joshua? Elena has made one of her Mexican specialties, I believe."

Garrett watched closely as Joshua moved at once to her boss's side. His touch on her elbow was polite, a courtly gesture that the independent woman couldn't possibly interpret as pity. The thoughtfulness behind his action pricked Garrett's conscience. Her own rudeness grated in the face of his good manners. She sighed as she watched Casey follow them into the dining room, chattering like a magpie until Mrs. Mac, chuckling, hushed her. "You're making my stomach hurt with your tall tales, girl. Elena will have our hides if we don't do justice to her dinner."

With Elena hovering, they sat down to enchiladas crammed with spicy chicken and doused liberally with sour cream. Refried beans and Spanish rice completed the main course. Garrett picked up the bowl of green chili salsa and spooned it sparingly on her food. Mrs. Mac shook her head when it was offered to her. Garrett turned to Joshua.

"Salsa?" she asked innocently.

"Of course."

He ladled on a generous portion that left Casey wide-eyed and Garrett chuckling to herself. He lifted the first forkful of food to his mouth. Garrett waited for him to grab for his glass of water. But even though the hot sauce brought tears to his eyes, he grinned. "Wonderful," he said with obviously genuine pleasure as Elena beamed, her face a roadmap of wrinkles. "This is the best Mexican food I've had since I lived in Texas. Most restaurants are real wimps about the seasonings."

"You lived in Texas?" Casey asked. "Did you have oil wells?"

"Afraid not."

"Cattle, like us?"

"No. My dad was a banker, first in ranching country,

then in Dallas. I guess I developed my fascination with numbers and money from listening to him. When banks all around us were failing, his stayed solvent.''

Casey seemed awed. "I'm flunking math," she admitted. "Numbers don't make any sense to me at all, especially algebra."

Joshua grinned at her. "Sounds to me like that's what we ought to have you studying on vacation, instead of chess," he said. "Numbers are great. You can always count on them to do the same thing."

There was an oddly sorrowful note in his voice that drew Garrett to ask, "What about people, Mr. Ames? Don't you trust them?"

He turned the full force of his gaze on her. She could feel the impact all the way to her toes and regretted drawing his attention to her. "Actually, I find certain people fascinating," he said in a low, seductive tone that made her pulse scamper like a newborn filly. "Tell me, how did you happen to end up on a Wyoming cattle ranch? Were you born around here?"

Garrett's mouth seemed to go dry under the intensity of his gaze. Fortunately her irrepressible daughter chimed in. "I was," she said. "But Mom moved here from Chicago before I was born. She worked in a diner as a waitress until Mrs. Mac hired her."

"Oh, really," he said, his eyes sparking with increased curiosity.

Garrett knew that look was about to lead to more questions. She tried to forestall them. "When did you and Cal meet?"

"When we were barely teenagers. My family moved into his neighborhood."

"So you roared through adolescence together."

"Cal roared. I grew up at a more sedate pace."

"Why was that?"

He shrugged as if the reason escaped him, but Garrett thought she detected a faint trace of some old hurt in the depths of his yes. "Were you rivals for the same girls?"

"No one was Cal's rival when it came to girls. They flocked to him."

"Don't be so modest," Mrs. Mac chided. "I imagine you had more than your share of feminine attention."

He grinned. "I have few complaints *now*, especially with Cal settled down and out of the running."

Garrett found the thought of Joshua Ames being pursued from coast to coast by glamorous women all too likely. He was probably the sort of rich, thoughtful, attentive lover who would appeal to any woman set on snagging a husband and challenged by his elusiveness. She wondered if any particular woman had the lead in capturing his heart. Because it infuriated her that the thought had even crossed her mind, there was a snap in her voice when she said, "Isn't it rather arrogant to assume you can take your pick of the remaining available women?"

Innocent blue eyes pinned her. "Is that what I said?"

"That's what it sounded like to me."

"Perhaps your hearing was affected by your own jealousy."

"It must be remarkably comforting to have an ego the size of yours, Mr. Ames."

Casey's gaze shot from Garrett to Joshua and back again. Even Mrs. Mac seemed taken aback by her sharp tone. Joshua simply laughed. "So I was right," he said. "You are jealous."

"I am not jealous," she said through gritted teeth. "Your love life is absolutely no concern of mine and I don't see that it's a fitting topic for conversation at the dinner table."

"You brought it up. Would you rather talk about your romantic conquests?"

"No, I would not."

Mrs. Mac appeared to be having trouble controlling a smile. "Now children," she said. "That's enough."

"Perhaps I'd better take my inflated ego back into the parlor, so I can get to work on those books," Joshua said.

"I wouldn't think of letting you work on your first night here," Mrs. Mac protested. "There will be plenty of time for straightening out those books tomorrow. Join us in the parlor for a nightcap."

Garrett very nearly groaned aloud when he blithely accepted the invitation. Still, to his credit, Joshua put on a polite facade for the next half hour. It seemed only Garrett was aware of the tension in the room. When she could stand it no longer, she excused herself.

"Casey and I really must be getting home. It's a school night."

Casey looked disappointed. She always enjoyed the chance to spend an evening with grown-ups. "But, Mom, I don't have any homework. Couldn't we stay a little longer?"

"Not tonight."

"Joshua, why don't you walk Garrett and Casey home?" Mrs. Mac suggested.

Garrett stared at her as if she'd suggested they fly to Acapulco together. "Really, that's not necessary," she said hurriedly.

"But it would be my pleasure," Joshua said, that spark of mischief back in his eyes. "I'll get my coat."

As soon as he'd left the room, Garrett whirled on Mrs. Mac. "It is less than a hundred yards to our house. I walk it alone every single night. Why did you suddenly decide we needed an escort?"

"It's always lovely to make a man think he's needed, Garrett. You really should remember that."

"This man is *not* needed," Garrett said, her voice strained.

Mrs. Mac regarded her with barely suppressed amusement. "Interesting," she observed.

After nearly ten years of working for the perceptive, outspoken cattlewoman, Garrett knew exactly what was going on in her head. "What's interesting?" she inquired reluctantly.

"The way you two get along."

"We don't."

"Exactly my point. Why is that, I wonder? You always get along with everybody. You're the most even-tempered person I've ever known. That's why you do so well with the hands. Not every woman could overcome the hands' natural distrust of female leadership, but the hands know they can count on you to be cool and objective under the worst kind of pressure."

Garrett squirmed under the penetrating gaze. "I guess I was due for a change."

"Hmm."

"Don't start with me, Mrs. Mac."

Mrs. McDonald looked as innocent as it was possible for an eighty-two-year-old maverick to look. "It was just an observation, my dear. There's no need to get huffy. Besides, it just proves my point," she said complacently.

"I am not getting huffy."

"Uh-huh."

Garrett scrambled to get into her coat. Half dragging Casey, she was almost at the door when Joshua reappeared.

"Leaving without me?" he inquired lightly.

Garrett sighed. "Of course not."

He beamed and an unwelcome shiver of anticipation zipped through her. When his hand settled in the middle of her back, it took everything in her to keep from jerking away. She would not give him the satisfaction of knowing that his touch affected her in any way. Nor would she create another scene in front of her highly impressionable daughter. As it was, Casey would be asking far too many discerning questions the instant they were alone.

Outside, with the crunch of snow under their feet, she took some satisfaction in the thought that the walk was ruining those expensive shoes of his. By the time they'd reached the door of the cozy house she and Casey shared, she had almost relaxed, lulled by the clear, starry beauty of the night and by Joshua's undemanding silence.

"Thank you," she said grudgingly.

His eyes twinkled. "Aren't you going to invite me in?"

Casey's mouth opened and slammed shut at a quick prod from Garrett's elbow. "Some other time," Garrett said.

Casey, who apparently had a greater sense of discretion than Garrett had ever had any reason to believe, slipped inside, leaving the two of them alone on the stoop.

Before she realized his intention, Joshua's hand was snug against her neck and his lips were against hers. The feather-light caress was undemanding and as potent as wine. Garrett's senses reeled, even as her anger rose. She opened her mouth to tell him just what she thought of his arrogant presumption, but he cleverly silenced her with yet another persuasive touch of his lips.

This time, lost to the hunger of the kiss, there was no denying the warmth that spread through her, the undeniable invitation in the way her body swayed toward his. For one tiny, fleeting moment she allowed herself the pure, feminine enjoyment of that greedy, demanding, thoroughly masculine possession.

Then she slugged him.

Chapter Three

Joshua had never been more startled in his life. His
jaw stung from the impact of Garrett's well-aimed
blow. Watching as acute embarrassment edged out fury
in her eyes, he began to chuckle. It had been years
since anyone had caught him off guard like that. He
gave her an admiring glance.

"Nice shot," he observed, rubbing his still-smarting
flesh.

"I'm sorry," she stammered, poking her hands into
her pockets and staring at the ground.

"Are you really?"

At his doubtful tone, her chin rose a defiant notch
and her eyes clashed with his. "No," she admitted.
"You deserved it."

"For kissing you?" he wondered. "Or because I made you want me?"

He was certain that not all of the sudden color in her cheeks could be attributed to the night air. "Don't flatter yourself," she snapped, but her heart obviously wasn't in it. They both knew she had wanted that kiss just as much as he had, and had probably been wondering about it every bit as long as he had.

He reached over and gently tapped her nose. "Remember the story of Pinnochio—terrible things happen to people who fib, especially when they lie to themselves."

Before she could respond, he turned and left. "Pleasant dreams," he called over his shoulder. He was all the way back at the main house before he heard the emphatic slam of her front door. He was laughing as he went inside.

By morning, he regretted being quite so cavalier. Nor was he quite as sure who'd had the last laugh. Overnight he had found himself giving the intriguing Traci Maureen Garrett considerable thought.

At midnight, he'd advised himself to cut his losses and ignore her.

At 1:00 a.m., he'd acknowledged that was impossible. He told himself she was like a burr that clung and irritated, then admitted she was more like pure temptation. The sweet hunger she'd tried so hard to hide was enough to lure a man to hell and hold him there.

By 3:00 a.m., he'd decided to take the first flight back to Florida, only to decide an hour later that he would not take the coward's way out. He'd left once before, when he should have stayed.

At five, he'd decided to spend the next few weeks pursuing her with every bit of all-out fervor at his command. The wickedly devilish scheme, admittedly, was dangerous. It was also the only plan likely to get her out of his system once and for all. Garrett was, no doubt, not the sort of woman who would wear well. He'd tire of her feisty, independent streak in no time. It never occurred to him to wonder what would happen if he didn't.

The decision rationally considered and made, he fell asleep at six, only to have her pester him relentlessly in his dreams. If her seductive behavior in that lone hour of sleep was any indication, he was about to embark on a suicide mission. Even so, he set out to find her first thing in the morning.

Seated in the parlor with Mrs. Mac, Garrett's cheeks were still pink from the wind and cold. Strands of golden hair had been tugged free from her braid to curl rebelliously about her face. She looked softer and more accessible than he'd ever seen her. Then she caught sight of him and that icy disdain that she used to distance herself wiped the smile from her lips.

"Good morning," Joshua said cheerfully, pointedly choosing the place next to her on the old love seat. Crowded beside her, he saw to it that their thighs brushed. Garrett's whole body stiffened, but she managed to resist her apparent desire to move away from his deliberate provocation.

Mrs. McDonald observed the subtle byplay closely, then beamed at him. "Good morning, young man. If you've decided to stay with us, you really must get warmer clothes. That shirt might do very nicely for an office in Florida, but out here you'll have pneumonia by the end of a week." She turned to Garrett. "Dear?"

Garrett blinked, as if her attention had been very far away—or perhaps mere inches, if she dared to be truthful. "Ma'am?" she said vaguely.

"I'd like you to go into Cheyenne with Joshua today. Show him where to get appropriate clothing. Put it on my account." She grinned at him. "I can charge that off as a business expense, can't I?"

"Not if I have anything to say about it."

"Then consider them an early Christmas gift."

"Really, it's not necessary."

"It is," she insisted, seemingly oblivious to the sudden strain in his voice. "Otherwise, you'll end up in the hospital and I'll have to come visit. This cold air is terrible for my old bones. You wouldn't want to put an old woman through all that pain, would you?"

"I suppose not," he said, unable to hold off the rush of familiar resentment at her kindly fussing. The reaction was all out of proportion to the gesture, but it was as ingrained as the multiplication tables. Echoes of his mother's voice resounded in his head. He started to protest, then saw the expectant gleam in Garrett's eyes and decided to remain silent. It was cold. The clothes he'd brought were inappropriate. Did it really matter who pointed it out or who paid for a couple of flannel shirts?

"Thank you," he said finally.

As if in some way she'd understood his internal struggle, Mrs. Mac didn't gloat. She merely nodded. "Good. Then that's settled."

"Not quite," Garrett said, obviously scrambling for an excuse now that he'd failed to provide her with a more convenient out. "I can't possibly drive into Cheyenne today. I have work to do."

Mrs. Mac waved aside the objection. "You have a dozen men out there who can do the work. I pay you to give them orders, which I'm sure you did at the crack of dawn as usual."

"You also pay me to see that they're carried out. What if there's a crisis?"

"There were crises on this ranch long before you arrived, my dear. I handled them. I suppose I can manage to rally for a few more."

Garrett immediately looked guilty. "I didn't mean..."

Mrs. Mac smiled. "I know you didn't, dear. We'll call Red in before you leave and you can give him any last-minute instructions." She waited for Garrett's reluctant nod, then moved briskly ahead. "Now that we're all agreed, why don't we have one last cup of coffee before you leave and I'll explain what else has to be done in Cheyenne. You might as well take care of a little business for me."

"Yes, why don't we do that?" Garrett said, her expression grim but resigned. She kept her gaze studiously fixed on her boss, ignoring Joshua. It was probably just as well, he thought. If she'd seen the blatant look of anticipation in his eyes, she probably would have slugged him again.

To stave off another blow, Joshua kept his own attention on Mrs. Mac's list of errands. Though he wouldn't have put it past her to contrive them, he had to admit they all sounded legitimate. She promised to write out careful, detailed instructions, along with appropriate notes for her banker and her attorney, guaranteeing that Joshua would get all the cooperation he needed to fully investigate the state of her business holdings.

"As long as you're here, I might as well take advantage of your expertise," she told him. "Garrett, there are one or two things you might want to take care of, as well."

The list went on and on. "Don't expect us back for dinner," Joshua said when he'd heard the last of her orders.

Garrett's startled gaze clashed with his. "We'll be back," she said with expected contrariness.

He placed his hand on her knee. "You really must let me thank you for all your trouble by taking you to dinner," he said emphatically.

"No thanks are necessary," she insisted, her teeth clenched.

"We'll discuss it on the way."

"The matter is settled."

"We'll see."

It was Mrs. Mac's chuckle that finally ended the debate. "Don't rush back. Enjoy yourselves," she said.

"Oh, I intend to," Joshua replied, his gaze lingering on Garrett's scowling face.

"You are impossible," she informed him twenty minutes later when they met outside. "Do you have to have everything your own way?"

"I'd be happy to accommodate your wishes," he said.

"Then leave me alone."

"This trip wasn't my idea."

"You could have told her no."

"She's my boss."

"Who are you kidding? You don't need her business. You're only here as a favor to Cal."

"I can't very well be rude to his grandmother, though, can I?"

"You'd be rude to God himself, if it suited your purposes. That must mean that this trip into Cheyenne suits your purposes. Would you mind telling me how?"

"I wanted to spend some time alone with you," he said bluntly.

She regarded him with frank skepticism. "Why?"

"You fascinate me."

Hands on her hips, obviously seething with indignation, she faced him. "Maybe we ought to get something clear now, Mr. Ames. I may live a simple life, but I wasn't born yesterday. I've met men like you before, rich men who think the whole world should be at their beck and call, callous men who don't give a damn about the feelings of the people they hurt. I am not about to become your personal toy while you're in town. If you're bored without your usual bevy of adoring women, then get your work done and go home.''

Joshua might have been stung by her analysis of his personality and integrity, but he was more intrigued by the story behind her anger. It was apparent to him that some man had hurt her deeply and for a surprising instant, he wanted to find him and beat him to a bloody pulp. The thought of trying to avenge Garrett's honor, when she had made it quite clear she could take care of herself, was amusing. It was made all the more ironic as he recalled all those infuriating years in his youth when he'd been too frail even to stand up for himself, and it had been Cal who'd come to his rescue more times than he cared to remember.

He owed Cal more than he could say for his staunch defense and for ultimately teaching him to defend himself. By the time he'd eventually rallied from the recurring childhood bouts with illness, he might have been resigned to being an unathletic weakling, but a fiercely protective Cal had seen to it that hadn't happened. He'd taught him to stand up to his overly protective mother and given him the skills to fend off bullies. Now, with regular workouts at the gym, he took his physical strength for granted. He'd be almost glad of the chance to use it to slay dragons for the woman who hid her vulnerability behind a facade of tough talk.

Instinctively wanting to help, he reached over and caressed her cheek. "Who hurt you?" he asked gently.

For a fraction of a second she seemed to be lost, caught up in the tenderness of his touch. Then she blinked away a faint sheen that might have been the start of tears and backed away. "We'll take the truck," she said matter-of-factly. "I'll drive."

"We'll take my car. I'll drive."

Garrett scowled. "Mr. Ames, this isn't some test of wills here. We're expecting more snow today. Your car won't be able to handle it." She directed a scathing glance at the convertible. "What on earth possessed you to rent something so unsuitable?"

"I like convertibles." He dropped his voice to a seductive murmur intended to play across her senses. "Haven't you ever ridden in one with the top down and the wind blowing through that long blond hair of yours, whipping it into your face?"

For an instant she looked almost wistful, then she said dryly, "Not when the windchill factor sets the temperature twenty degrees below freezing and there's snow in the air."

He shivered at the reminder. "You have a point. Okay. We'll take the truck, but I'll drive."

"It's straight shift."

"That's the only kind we rich playboys drive," he mocked, finally getting a smile from her.

She handed him the keys. "You win, hotshot, but when the blizzard starts, don't beg me for help."

"I wouldn't dream of it. Besides, the prospect of a

blizzard raises all sorts of interesting possibilities for tonight.''

"You must have a really rich fantasy life, Mr. Ames."

He smiled. "It's getting better all the time."

They saved the shopping for last. It was probably just as well. Garrett wasn't at all certain she was going to survive the impact of seeing Joshua emerge from a dressing room in jeans, a Western shirt and boots. It didn't seem to matter that the boots had a spit-polish shine or that the jeans were still stiff. If the man had been perched on a barstool in Angel Dawson's saloon, she'd have labeled him a cowboy. A devilishly handsome cowboy, she admitted ruefully, as whipcord lean and hard as any one of the hands at the ranch.

"What do you think?" he asked.

"You'll do."

"That's the best you can come up with?" he retorted, sounding genuinely disappointed.

Garrett found herself grinning. He reminded her of the five-year-old Casey dressed in one of Garrett's fancy Sunday dresses, lipstick smeared across her face, her tiny feet tucked into Garrett's high-heeled shoes. That same hopeful expression had been in her eyes when she'd said, "Mommy, how do I look? Am I as pretty as you?"

Remembering that, she patted Joshua's arm. "You're very handsome," she conceded. "There's just one thing missing." She walked over to a display of cowboy hats, picked out a black one and brought it back.

"I thought the good guys wore white," he responded.

"They do," she said, standing on tiptoe to settle the black one on his head at a rakish angle. As she leaned into him, her breasts brushed his chest and her breath snagged in her throat. Breathless, she felt herself trapped by the intensity of his gaze and the utter stillness that fell over him. Expectation pulsed between them. With the hat in place, she suddenly seemed unable to figure out what to do with her hands. As if they had a will of their own, they dropped to his chest, lingering for no more than a heartbeat, just long enough to feel the thudding of his heart, to take in the vitality and warmth his body promised.

As if she'd taken a dare, only to discover that the price was way too high, she jerked her hands away. "We'd better be going."

Regret shadowed his eyes, but he nodded agreeably. She was so busy being thankful because he didn't argue that she wasn't prepared to have him hurry her from the store straight down the sidewalk and into a restaurant they'd passed earlier. She balked at the door, but the scent of spices, the cozy warmth of a fireplace and Joshua's hand firmly on her back propelled her inside.

"We should leave now, before the snow gets any worse," she said.

It was a sensible suggestion, but she delivered it so mildly she couldn't really blame him for ignoring it.

The real truth of the matter was that she didn't want to go. The air of anticipation that had been flirting with her senses ever since Joshua's arrival the previous afternoon was having an odd effect on her. After all these years, she was remembering what it was like to have her blood run wild and feverishly. She was rediscovering the thrill of being desired. And, she admitted, she wasn't ready for it to end quite yet. A nice restaurant seemed like the perfect place to indulge herself in Joshua's attention without any threat of an intimacy she couldn't handle.

She flirted outrageously, watching the flare of heat in his eyes with feminine satisfaction. When his fingers skimmed across hers, she tried to analyze why such an innocent touch could make her pulse race, then gave up and simply enjoyed the effect. With every sip of wine, she became less cautious. It had been so long since Garrett had played with fire, she'd forgotten the risks of getting burned. They were halfway home when it came to her exactly what kind of trouble she'd gotten herself into by permitting the lingering, provocative dinner. The wind was howling. The snow was falling in billowing, blinding whirls, coating the road with windblown drifts. It might have been beautiful, if it hadn't been so dangerous. Tension immediately replaced her mellow mood.

"Have you ever driven in snow like this before?" she asked, noticing that Joshua's knuckles were white as his hands gripped the steering wheel.

"No."

"Then let me drive the rest of the way."

For an instant she thought he'd say no just to prove how macho he was, but he glanced over at her and nodded. "You're probably right. You know more about handling a truck in this stuff than I do."

He pulled to the side of the road and traded places with her.

"Thank you," she said.

"For what?"

"For not being a jerk about this."

"I'm not interested in getting the two of us killed just to prove some ridiculous point."

Just then the truck skidded wildly. Garrett fought against every instinct and turned into the skid. Once the truck was under control again she risked a glance at Joshua. He looked perfectly calm.

"No sarcastic comments?" she asked disbelievingly.

"We're still on the road, aren't we? I'd have had us in the ditch."

"Don't give me too much blind trust. We're still twenty-five miles from home and this storm is getting worse by the minute."

Joshua peered out the fogged-over windshield. "I don't see how you can tell where the hell we are. It all looks the same to me."

"That's because you're used to watching for street signs instead of landmarks." She pointed toward a faint shadow on the left. "That's Bear Claw over there. Just up ahead you'll be able to see a stand of cottonwoods. They're right alongside Horse Creek."

"All I see is white."

To be perfectly honest that was nearly all Garrett could see, as well, but she figured there was no sense in both of them panicking. If she could make it another three miles or so, they'd be within hiking distance of an old line cottage on the edge of Tom Rutgers's ranch. If they had to, they could stay there for the night. It wouldn't be fancy, but it would be stocked with provisions and wood for a fire. They'd survive. With the snow this bad, no one at home would be expecting them anyway. If she hadn't been so muddleheaded with wine and other distractions, she would never have left Cheyenne in this weather.

Just then, she noticed the headlights bearing down on them, coming far too fast for a road this slick. She pressed lightly on the brake as she steered toward the shoulder of the road, trying to give the idiot room enough to pass. For an instant she thought they'd be just fine.

Then, suddenly, the truck lost traction. They hit a rut and skidded straight toward a ditch.

"Hang on," she warned tightly. "It's going to be a bumpy ride."

She heard Joshua's low chuckle. "Seems to me Bette Davis once said that."

"Yes, but she wasn't about to crash into a ditch."

Garrett struggled with the steering wheel, but it was apparent that the truck wasn't going to stay on the road. She eased up on the brakes, figuring the best she could hope for now was to lessen the jolt when they skidded to a stop. Fortunately they were in no real danger of smashing into anything. Nor was the ditch so deep that they were likely to flip.

With one last jarring bounce, they rocked to a stop. Her arms tense and aching from trying to maintain control of the truck, she leaned forward and rested her head against the steering wheel.

She felt Joshua's fingers against her cheek, the touch gentle and comforting. "Are you okay?"

"Just embarrassed."

She risked a glance in his direction and discovered he was grinning. Either he was oblivious to their plight or he was just plain nuts. Maybe he'd hit his head.

"If I'd known how badly you wanted to spend the night alone with me, I'd have suggested a room in Cheyenne," he teased.

"This is no time to be joking. We're in a mess of trouble. People freeze to death in weather like this."

"Surely not cowgirls."

"I'm serious, Joshua. We're a long way from the nearest shelter. We can't stay in the truck with the heater on. That's a good way to suffocate, too."

"Maybe help will come along."

"The only people on the road tonight are idiots, like that guy who ran us off."

"Or like us."

She frowned. "Like I said, idiots."

"Hey, we made a bad call. Now we're stuck in a ditch. Moaning about it won't save our necks. Maybe we can get the truck out. I'll check it out."

Garrett didn't want to admit that she was impressed with his totally unflappable attitude. It might be foolhardy, but it was certainly better than the hysterical accusations he might have been flinging in her face. As he climbed out of the truck, Garrett shivered in the blast of icy air. She knew what he was going to find, but if it made him feel better to see that they were well and truly stranded, so be it. It was no time at all before the door opened again. Joshua's expression was grimmer now.

"Can you find your way to that shelter?"

Garrett nodded halfheartedly, realizing that she'd been hoping against hope that she was wrong about their plight. "I can try." She took a deep breath, then added somberly, "If we get lost, Joshua, we could die of exposure. That's a very real risk on a night like this."

"And the odds of us dying right here?"

"Depends on how long the storm lasts or whether somebody finally does come along."

"I vote we try to make it to the shelter. You?"

Still amazed that he wasn't casting blame, she decided if they ever got out of this fix she might have to re-evaluate her impression of his gumption. "Let's go. There are flashlights and blankets in the back. I'll leave a flare in the snow, so if anyone does come along and see the truck they'll call for help."

"Too bad this truck doesn't have a radio. I'd think anyone driving the distances you all do out here would find that a necessity."

"We do," she admitted ruefully. "This one's in for repair. There's probably one in Rutgers's shack, though. Once we get there, we'll be able to let everyone know where we are."

She saw him smiling at her. "What's so amusing?"

"Not amusing. Impressive. Now that we've made the decision, you have no doubts at all that we'll make it, do you?"

She turned the bravest smile she could manage on him. "With what we've got ahead of us, doubts could be a real killer."

Joshua held out his hand. "Then let's go for a hike in the snow, sweetheart. I can't think of anything more romantic."

Garrett scowled. "Doesn't your mind ever veer away from sex?"

"Doesn't yours?" he challenged. "I was talking about romance, not sex."

"Sure you were."

The argument might have gotten even more heated if they hadn't needed every single whisper of breath just to go on.

Chapter Four

The killer was the bitter, biting wind. It cut through all their layers of clothing, aided by the dampness of the snow that clung to their faces, to their hair, to their coats. Drifts, some already hip-high, hampered their slow, tedious, slippery progress along the roadway.

They'd been walking for nearly an hour and it was virtually impossible to tell how far they'd gone. Surrounded by endless whiteness, they could barely see to take the next step. By staying carefully on the road, they'd cut the risk of getting lost or wandering in circles. However, with fresh snow filling their tracks almost the instant they'd moved on, it was as if they'd gone nowhere, as if they'd never been at all. Joshua had to wonder if anyone finding the truck would even be able to track them.

"You look like a snowman," Garrett observed with a thready laugh that hinted she was near hysteria.

Joshua stopped and drew her into a tight embrace meant to comfort and warm, if only slightly. Surprised that she didn't resist, he gazed into her eyes. Almost at once he became caught up in the unexpected vulnerability he found in the blue depths in that one unguarded instant. The woman in his arms at this moment was a woman he could love, a woman he could cherish and protect always. The realization stunned him.

Drawn to Garrett as never before, he pressed his lips to her cold, wet cheek, to her forehead, her eyelids, then her cheek again before settling inevitably on her trembling mouth. She tasted of snowflakes, but the heat that raged through him felt as if he'd stirred the embers of a dying fire. Though only temporary, he prayed it would be enough to keep them both going.

"You look beautiful," he whispered, staring into eyes now shining with unshed tears.

"I'm sorry," she said, her gloved fingers against his face.

"For what? Dumping us into a drift?"

"No. For thinking..." Her teeth chattered uncontrollably. "For thinking you were a jerk."

"Sometimes I am."

She shook her head adamantly. "No."

"Something tells me you won't think quite so kindly of me once you've had a chance to get warm again and come to your senses. If it weren't so damned cold out here, I'd be tempted to take advantage of your attitude while it lasts."

She shivered, but managed a faint smile. "Once a lecher, always a lecher," she said with a sigh that feathered against his cheek.

"If you wanted a gentleman out here with you, you came with the wrong guy."

She tilted her chin and examined him thoughtfully. "Mrs. Mac thinks you're a gentleman."

"Hey, no fair," he said, tucking her arm through his and beginning to move ahead again. "Women always throw around compliments like that just to trap a man into behaving the way they want him to."

"What?"

"You know exactly what I mean. *I know how much you respect me; I just know I can trust you.* What man would dare to try seducing a woman who's just said that? It would make him into the worst sort of sleeze."

"I'll have to remember that," she said softly, the words slurring slightly.

She stumbled over a thick branch buried deep in the snow and fell to her knees. Joshua lifted her up and prodded her on. The weariness in her voice terrified him. Surviving in a blizzard was beyond his experience, but he knew he didn't dare let her fall asleep. "Come on, lady. We have miles to go before we sleep."

"But I'm so tired," she protested. "Couldn't we rest for just a minute?"

"I'm tired, too, but I don't relish a snowbank for a

pillow. Look around. See any of those famous land-marks you recognize? We've been following the road for over an hour now. On a good day that would mean about four or five miles at least. Tonight it's no more than a couple. Is there anything closer than the shack you mentioned?''

She shuddered so hard, her whole body shook. "No-o-o. No-o-thing."

"Then we'll keep going. Why don't you tell me about Chicago? I've always liked it there. Why on earth would you ever leave?"

Her expression altered at once. An unforgiving chill turned her eyes as icy as their surroundings. "I—I h-hated it."

Sensing that he'd touched on a nerve that could stir her blood with anger, he pushed. "Why?"

Her gaze skittered away evasively. "I—I just did."

"But the drive along Lake Michigan is beautiful. There's so much to do—theater, art, restaurants, shopping in the Loop or Watertower Place. All women love to shop. You left that behind for this?" He waved his hand at the snowy spread of lonely emptiness.

She glared at him and to his relief he could practically feel the heat rising inside her.

"Mind you, I'm not thrilled with the fix we're in right now," she said, "but I'd take this over Chicago any day. The skies are endless washes of blue. There's no crowding, no city crime, no deep-down dirt. Life here is so uncomplicated. The people are honest and decent and hardworking. When I was a little girl, I used to dream of places like this. I couldn't wait to come.''

"Casey said you worked in a diner when you first got out here.''

"I waited tables, did a little cooking until the customers rebelled at my burnt toast. The couple who owned it were kind. They didn't ask a lot of questions about my past.''

He heard the hint of censure in her voice, but it only spurred his curiosity. "What kind of past could an eighteen-year-old girl possibly have had that she'd want to hide?''

She didn't reply for so long that he thought he'd gone too far. Finally, her voice faint but defiant, she said, "I was sure you'd guessed by now. I was pregnant.''

Left unspoken was the fact that she'd obviously been unmarried, as well, and that she was still deeply ashamed. He wished with everything in him that he'd been around to protect her back then, to claim her and Casey as his own.

"You aren't the first woman to make a mistake,'' he reminded her gently.

"Casey was not a mistake,'' she said fiercely. "I love her. She's the very best thing in my life.''

He squeezed her hand tightly. "Sweetheart, I know that. Anyone seeing the two of you together would know it. But at eighteen you were alone and scared. It must have been hard for you.''

"It was hard and it was lonely, but it was heaven compared to what I'd left behind."

She pulled her hand free and lurched on ahead, obviously desperate to put distance between them. Questions raced through Joshua's mind, but this time he wisely kept them to himself. Probing Garrett's secrets, understanding how she had become the pricklish, solitary woman she was today were not on tonight's agenda. Tonight was all about survival, getting the two of them to that cabin before this hateful blizzard froze them to death. If nothing else, he had touched a nerve so sensitive that the fire of her anger would keep her going awhile longer.

Garrett hated remembering. She had spent too many years forgetting, setting up a dam against the inevitable tide of hurt. Yet no matter how hard she tried, the memories always flooded back. Every time they did, they were just as fresh, just as painful as they'd been on the day she'd caught the bus west from Chicago. Right now, hip-deep in another drift of snow, she hated Joshua for making her remember. She wanted to get as far from his penetrating questions as she could.

It was only when she'd covered another half mile or so with him trudging silently behind her that she realized he'd purposely goaded her. He'd given her the incentive to keep going when her whole body had wanted to sink into nothingness.

The irony, of course, was that the farther she went, the closer she came to the time when they would be alone in that cabin with no way left for her to avoid the probing questions about her past. She could retreat into stubborn, defiant silence, but she had a feeling Joshua knew exactly how to get around a woman's resistance. If she didn't want to talk, he'd suggest occupying her time with something far more intimate and dangerous. Every kiss they'd shared told her that she'd be far better off talking, gabbing until she was blue in the face. She'd be wise to tell him about the cattle, about Casey, about Wyoming, even about the past, if only it would keep the undeniable, growing attraction between them safely at bay.

Realistically, though, she knew there weren't enough words in the world to do that. As miserably cold as she was, she had only to look into his eyes to feel a stirring of heat. She had only to feel the strong clasp of his gloved hand around her own to feel warmth spreading through her. His kisses exploded into welcome fire.

And that meant trouble. She knew it as well as she knew that another hour out in this weather and she'd have more to worry about than the effect of a few stolen kisses. It was unbearably cold. In all the years she'd lived in Wyoming, she had never been exposed for this long to the bone-chilling iciness. Her feet and hands were dangerously numb, probably close to frost-bitten.

Still, they trudged on, Joshua keeping up a running patter of nonsensical, one-sided conversation. At least she assumed it was nonsensical. She couldn't seem to concentrate on what he was saying. She only wanted to sleep, to hibernate like a bear until this awful storm ended and spring emerged to turn the prairie grasslands an undulating green.

"Garrett. Garrett! Come on, sweetheart. You have to pay attention."

Joshua's words seemed to reach her through a thick fog. "Pay attention to what?" she said finally, because he seemed to expect her to say something.

"The landmarks. What should we be looking for?"

"Trees. Cottonwoods. The creek. It'll be frozen now." She tilted her face up to catch a snowflake on the tip of her tongue. For a moment she forgot to be afraid, forgot that she was with the man who threatened her peace of mind. She was a child again and the world was a beautiful, magical fairyland. "Do you skate, Joshua? We could go ice-skating on the creek."

"If you ask me, we're already skating on thin ice. This is about as dangerously as I care to live."

"I could teach you to do a figure eight. Mrs. Mac taught me."

He regarded her incredulously. "You and Mrs. Mac went ice-skating?"

"It was the first year I was at the ranch. Casey was only a baby, so it must have been..." She tried to make the calculations, but the numbers seemed to be elusive. "A long time ago. Mrs. Mac loved to skate. She said it reminded her of when she and her husband were courting. He drank himself to death. Did you know that? Then her daughter, Cal's mother, ran away and married a man Mrs. Mac didn't approve of. It was very sad."

She felt the sting of sympathetic tears in her eyes. "Did you know she's been running this ranch by herself for nearly fifty years? She's even been president of the cattlemen's association. Isn't it nice the way women are respected in Wyoming? They always have been, you know. They got the vote here really early. It's probably because men saw how well they coped with the hard life here. Women are much tougher than men think."

She cast a curious gaze in Joshua's direction, wondering what his reaction would be to that declaration. "Well?" she insisted. "What do you think?"

"About what?" he said distractedly.

"About women?"

"I'm rather partial to them." An unmistakable gleam lit his eyes.

"That is not what I asked you. I asked if you agreed that we're tougher than men think we are?"

"I think you are very tough."

She smiled. "Thank you."

"Of course, I think your brain is freezing."

She regarded him indignantly. "It is not."

"Then explain to me why we are having this ridiculous conversation, when I need you to help me find that line shack."

"I am helping."

"How?"

That was a tough one. So far, he was the one who'd kept them moving. "I'm watching for the trees."

"Any sign of them?"

"No," she admitted dejectedly. "Actually, I'm really tired, Joshua."

"I know you are, sweetheart, but it's bound to be close. Is it on the road?"

"No. It's a few hundred yards to the east."

Joshua groaned. "Then how the hell are we supposed to see it from the road?"

"I keep telling you about the trees. Aren't you listening?" she replied testily.

"I don't see any damn trees."

Challenged, Garrett peered through the blinding, whirling snow. She could barely see Joshua, much less anything at a distance. His doubts, however, had given her the incentive to keep going. She would prove to him, prove to all of them that women were tough, that *she* was tough. She'd been trying to prove it her whole life.

Drawing on her last reserves of energy, she plowed on through the snow, knowing that they had to be close, fearing that if they didn't find the cabin soon, she and Joshua would become one of those tragic cases of people who died of exposure only a few feet from warmth and protection.

Now it was Joshua who was lagging behind, dispirited. It was up to her to save them now. He had gotten them this far by badgering and cajoling. The tactics had been underhanded but clever. Once again she admitted she was going to have to revise her initial impression of Joshua. He might be a greenhorn, but he had a streak of inventiveness and determination in him she had to admire. She wondered if he would be equally as resourceful as a lover. She flirted with the idea for several minutes and decided the possibilities were fascinating. Wasn't it odd, how he'd started her thinking about sex? She'd studiously avoided thinking about it for a long time now. Garrett glanced sideways and caught his bleak expression. This was no time to be indulging in impossible fantasies, she reminded herself sternly.

"I think I see the trees," she lied, using hope as an incentive.

"Where?"

"Just ahead. Come on, Joshua. We're almost there."

"There are no trees."

"Damn it, I see them," she insisted. "Walk."

"I am walking."

"Faster. It'll keep your blood circulating."

"I wonder if the stories are true," he said.

"What stories?"

"About people who've frozen to death coming back to life once they've thawed out."

"I will not allow you to think like that," she said furiously. "We are not going to freeze to death. We are not going to require thawing out."

He turned a silly, endearing grin on her. "I'd enjoy thawing you out, Garrett."

She moaned at his craziness, but she couldn't deny that the mere suggestion had sent a gentle wave of heat washing through her. Definitely a resourceful lover, she decided, intrigued again by the thought. If the image stirred her blood, maybe it would do the same for his.

"What is the first thing you're going to do when we find the cabin?" she said.

"Build a fire."

"And then?"

"Get out of these wet clothes."

That aroused some provocative images. She was getting warmer by the second.

"And then?"

He regarded her intently. Heat was definitely flaring in his eyes. She congratulated herself as he asked, "Are you deliberately leading me on here?"

"Leading you on?" she repeated innocently.

"Planting seductive little notions in my mind just to turn up my thermostat?"

"Would I do that?"

"You would if you thought it would motivate me to keep going."

"Is it working?"

"It's working, sweetheart. If my body ever gets as hot as my thoughts, you're in a whole pile of trouble."

The prospect might have daunted her but just then she saw the landmark they'd been watching for, the stand of trees and the creek just beyond.

"Joshua," she breathed softly, reaching out to clasp his hand.

He went absolutely still beside her. "What?"

"We've found it!"

''The cabin?'' he said doubtfully, peering through the curtain of snow that fell before them.

''The creek, but the cabin won't be far now.'' Impulsively she threw her arms around him. ''We made it, Joshua! It's okay. In no time we'll be in front of that fire.''

She looked up then and caught the blaze in his eyes. Suddenly reality caught up with seductive fantasy. She realized what she had done by planting all those provocative possibilities in his head...and in her own. He'd pretty well summed it up, in fact. She was in a whole pile of trouble.

Chapter Five

Never in his life had Joshua been so relieved to see a primitive little snowbound shack in the middle of nowhere. Half buried in snow and totally unprepossessing, it was as welcome as any suite in any five-star hotel he'd ever visited in some exciting world capital.

The last hour had been pure hell. He'd been terrified that Garrett was going to give up before they reached safety. Then he'd been struck by a sudden inspiration. He'd guessed that she would rally if he challenged her, if he made it a test of her fortitude against his. For some reason she seemed to feel a deep need to prove herself to him, to declare her independence and strength at every turn. Discovering why could prove to be fascinating, if only he could stop this violent shivering long enough to put his mind to the task.

"We're going to have to break in," he said, already looking around for something heavy to use on one of the narrow windows. They'd have to patch it later to keep the cold out.

"No, it'll be unlocked. It's left that way specifically for emergencies like this. We just have to get to the door."

Even that appeared a daunting prospect with drifts blocking their way. "I don't suppose you have a folding shovel tucked in your back pocket?" he asked.

"Afraid not."

"Then let's get to work."

With stiff hands that would barely do his bidding, he scooped away snow that was piled halfway up the cabin door. Garrett worked silently beside him until at last they were able to get to the handle and push the door open. Snow trailed in behind them and the vicious gusts of wind made closing the door again almost impossible. They both put their weight against it to slam it closed.

Only when it was shut did he think to ask, "Is the firewood outside?"

Her shoulders sagging with fatigue, Garrett nodded. "Probably buried in that drift. There should be some in the fireplace, though. Let's get a fire started and warm up some before we bring in more." Her gaze turned hopefully toward the stone hearth.

Joshua shook his head. "I'll get it now. Once I settle down, I'm not going to be the least bit interested in braving that weather again before morning."

"You won't have long to wait. It's nearly morning now."

"It can't be. It was barely midnight when the car went into that ditch."

She glanced at her watch. "And it's 4:00 a.m. now. By all rights we should have frozen to death in that time." She shuddered. "If you hadn't kept us going..."

He shook his head and clasped her hands. His eyes met hers. "I'd say we're even." The tension that had sprung to life every single time they'd touched crackled through the air again, until at last he said softly, "Why don't you start a fire and see if there's coffee or some brandy? I'll get more wood."

Bracing himself against the wind, he went back outside. As Garrett had suspected, there was a supply of logs just outside, covered with snow. He carried three loads inside and would have gone back for a fourth if Garrett hadn't suggested with a wry expression that they had enough for the next twenty-four hours.

"I want a big fire."

"You'll warm up quickly enough," she promised as she knelt before the hearth and touched a match to the kindling. The first spark held the promise of a blazing warmth that drew him to her side. He held his still-gloved hands toward the flames and felt the tingling pain that came as his circulation was restored.

"You can lose the gloves," she teased. "Now they're just keeping the heat out." She reached over and removed them for him. Again, her gaze caught his and held. Her fingers, every bit as stiff and icy as his own, skimmed over the back of his hands. He captured them and held on.

"Your hands are frozen," she said.

"So are yours." He touched his lips to her fingers. "Does that help?"

Slowly she nodded.

He placed her hands inside his jacket, against his chest. "And that?"

A faint tremor swept through her, but again she nodded.

"What about the rest of you? How do you feel?"

"I can't even feel my feet."

"Let's take a look," he said, releasing her hands. "Sit right here in front of the fire." She huddled on the braided rug, her shoulders hunched over her knees as he reached for her boots and tugged them off. "Wiggle your toes."

She stared at her feet, an expression of consternation on her face. Nothing happened. "I think they're too stiff to wiggle," she said finally.

Joshua picked up one icy foot and began to rub, trying hard to ignore the effect that touching her was having on him. For a man who was half frozen, he was having decidedly overheated thoughts. Since those thoughts were about as out of place tonight as he was in this cabin, he concentrated instead on Garrett's poor, icy feet.

Think of it as a medical emergency, he told his straying libido. The truth of that had absolutely no impact.

Instead he found himself fascinated by the incongruity of a woman who ran a cattle ranch and prided herself on tough, fiery independence wearing a frosty-pink toenail polish. Sexiness hidden by rawhide, vulnerability protected by cactus prickliness. It seemed to sum up her whole intriguing personality.

As if she sensed the direction of his thoughts, Garrett drew away from him. "They're better now," she said. "Why don't you check to see if there are some dry clothes we can put on, while I make that coffee?"

The last thing Joshua wanted to do right that second was put on clothes. With an intensity that rocked him, he realized he was much more interested in getting the rest of Garrett's clothes off. He wanted her with a blaze of raw desire that could have heated the whole damned cabin. The force of his yearning was compounded by the certainty that he shouldn't take her, not tonight, maybe not ever. There were too many complications, too many unanswered questions. He'd discovered the depths of his own feelings tonight, but he had no idea what he should do about them. As for Garrett, he couldn't even begin to guess what she was thinking, what she was feeling.

Oh, she wanted him. He had few doubts about that. But she would have regrets in the morning and even deeper ones after he'd gone. Some instinct warned him that she'd been left once too often in the past. Joshua wouldn't be the one to do it to her again and until he'd given it a lot more thought, he couldn't promise her that wouldn't happen.

To take his mind off the needs his body had expressed in plain, masculine language, he looked around the single room and decided that calling it a shack was a serious misnomer. Though it was small, it was well equipped for emergencies or for those times when cowboys were chasing cattle far from the bunkhouse. A lone, narrow bed, made up with white sheets and layers of colorful wool blankets, was pushed against one wall. A sofa, which likely converted to a bed, had been placed in front of the fire and a small kitchen area included a refrigerator, well-stocked cupboards, a stove and a rough-hewn table with two chairs. A well-used deck of cards on the table was testimony to the late-night pursuits of the last occupants and curtains at the windows suggested a woman's touch in this man's domain. There was no sign of a telephone or radio. The cabin's one other door led, he hoped, to a bathroom.

Before investigating that, he opened a trunk at the foot of the bed and found several flannel shirts, neatly folded, along with a pair of jeans. He held the pants next to his body and decided they were probably an inch or two short, but they'd do. He went into the bathroom, took a shower in surprisingly hot water, dressed and then took another of the shirts to Garrett.

"Go change. I'll watch the coffee."

While she was gone, he found cups, then hunted in the cupboards for a can of soup. It had been hours since dinner and they needed to get something more into them besides caffeine. He dumped the chicken noodle soup into a pot and turned on the heat. He'd just gotten bowls out when he sensed that Garrett was back in the room. He turned and saw her standing in front of the fire and suddenly his breath turned ragged.

Her hair was no longer braided and the golden waves fell halfway down her back like a splash of sunlight. The flannel shirt skimmed over curves to end just above her knees, leaving a provocative amount of slim, bare legs to tempt a man. Deliberately turning his back on her, he said in a choked voice, "Maybe you ought to wrap yourself in one of those blankets."

"I'm fine. It's plenty warm in here now."

Warm. It was maybe five degrees cooler than hell itself. All of Joshua's good intentions had been shot down with one glimpse of those heavenly, long legs. Those legs could wrap around a man and hold him prisoner until he drowned in a sea of wild sensations. Images, dangerous images, flashed through his mind, lingered, tempted and then were determinedly banished. Only to return again. And again.

A smart man would go outside and fling himself facedown in the snow. A wise man would sit down at this kitchen table with a cup of coffee and a bowl of soup and forget all about temptation, if he had to methodically count noodles to do it. Joshua told himself all about being smart and wise as he crossed the room and stood beside her. When she turned to face him, her cheeks flushed from the fire, her hair shimmering, his heart slammed against his ribs. God, she was gorgeous, desirable.

"Even after everything we've been through tonight, you look beautiful," he said, his voice husky.

She lifted her head and hesitant, troubled eyes met his. She took a deep breath, then blurted, "Joshua, I've been thinking."

"About?"

"We're stuck here for the rest of the night, maybe even longer."

"Yes."

"I don't want you to think...I mean, just because we're alone here..."

"I'm not going to do anything you don't want me to do," he said, brushing a strand of still-damp hair from her face, his fingertips lingering against the flushed, soft-as-silk skin.

"No. Of course not," she said hurriedly. "It's just that I think things should be clear."

She was being so serious, so intent. His lips twitched in amusement. "Absolutely."

"So I'll sleep on the sofa," she announced firmly.

"You'll sleep in the bed."

"You can't possibly sleep on that sofa. It's too short."

"It probably converts to a bed."

"It doesn't."

"I'll manage." He grinned. "Unless, of course, you could be persuaded to share."

Her expression clouded over. "Didn't you hear a word I just said?"

"All of them, as a matter of fact. Soup?" He went

back to the kitchen area and began ladling the soup into the bowls, telling himself it was a damned good thing one of them had some willpower. He sure as hell didn't.

"We really need to talk about this," she insisted.

"Why? It's all settled. You sleep in the bed. I sleep on the sofa. It's only one night, after all. I've slept on worse." He couldn't actually recall when. "Eat your soup."

"I don't want the damned soup. I want to discuss this."

"Why? Is there some reason you're obsessed with our sleeping arrangements? If you want, I could put a cord down the middle of the room and drape a blanket over it. They did that in a movie once. Of course, it was back in the thirties or forties."

"If you're implying that I'm being old-fashioned and prudish—"

"If the shoe fits."

"I just think it's better to spell things out from the beginning, so there are no misunderstandings."

"The winner of the National Spelling Bee couldn't have done it any better. Your soup's getting cold."

Glaring at him, she sat down at the kitchen table and began to eat. The silence throbbed with tension, a sexual awareness that all of his glib words and her rules hadn't cooled one whit. Damn it! In her attempts to warn him off, she'd only succeeded in making him want her more. Whatever happened between now and morning, he could not sit by and watch her crawl into that lonely single bed. It would be such a terrible waste. It would also be sheer torture.

He picked up the deck of cards and shuffled. Suddenly he was propelled back thirty years, to the endless days when he'd been confined to bed with nothing more than a game of solitaire between him and awful, mind-numbing boredom. With a glint in his eyes, he dealt the cards.

"Five card stud," he announced tersely.

"Joshua, I'm exhausted."

He glanced significantly across the room. Her gaze followed his, saw the now-controversial bed and returned to the cards before her. Picking them up, she glanced over them, chose two decisively and dropped them on the table.

His eyebrows rose. "Just two?"

"Two," she confirmed, her expression grim.

They played until the cabin began to fill with the first muted light of dawn. Garrett yawned, glanced at the score sheet she'd insisted on keeping and announced, "You owe me four thousand, seven hundred and twenty-six dollars." She squinted at the paper. "And thirty-two cents."

"You cheat."

A smile teased at the corners of her mouth. "Joshua, you do not tell a cowboy he's cheating at cards unless you have proof or a gun."

"Then it's a good thing you're a girl, isn't it?"

She frowned at once. "A *cowgirl*," she corrected. "And I may not have a shotgun with me, but I would hate to have to tell Mrs. Mac that you're the kind of man who welshes on his debts. She has a shotgun."

"By her bed. Yes, I know. She told me. You realize, of course, that I wouldn't be a bit of use to her if she shot me."

"Her aim's pretty good. You'd still be able to add and subtract."

"I'm not so sure that's all she has in mind for me."

"Meaning?"

"I think she has plans for the two of us."

Pink stole into Garrett's cheeks. "I can't imagine what gave you that idea, but you're absolutely wrong."

"I don't think so. She'll probably be waiting for us with that shotgun, but not for the reason you think. She'll probably insist on my marrying you now that I've besmirched your honor by spending an entire night alone with you in this cabin."

"I'm sure you'll be the first to correct her impression."

He grinned. "I don't know. My masculine pride's at stake here, too."

She tossed her cards on the table and stood up. "Go to hell," she said with feeling.

He got slowly to his feet and leaned across the table until he was within mere inches of her delectable mouth. "But this is so much more fun," he said, his gaze locked on her lips. His breath snagged. "Damn it, I want you, Garrett," he said, his voice a mixture of regret and yearning.

"It's not me you want," she said, but she didn't back away.

He was touched by the haunted look in her eyes. He told himself that she needed proof, longed for it, but would never in a thousand years admit it.

"It is you I want," he said emphatically. Cupping her chin in his hand, he proved it by touching his lips to hers. "So soft," he murmured. "So sweet."

Her mouth trembled and her eyes suddenly lit with a flare of pure longing. In one swift move he shoved the table aside and drew her to him, claiming her mouth with a hunger that raged through him like wildfire. All the fears of the previous night fueled him with desperation. He could have lost her, lost himself without ever knowing the sweetness of her, without ever savoring the way she was melting in his arms.

By the time his fingers looped under the hem of the flannel shirt, she had abandoned herself to the feelings she'd kept banked through the night. Shyness and self-denial seemed to vanish on a wave of passion that took them both by surprise with its primitive force of raw need.

"Hurry," she told him when his fingers found her heat at last. She arched her back, moving against his hand, pleading with him. "Joshua, please hurry. Please."

With slow deliberation, he pulled back. "Not yet. Not yet."

Not until he could strip away the shirt that hid her from his gaze. Not until he could take the rosy tip of each full breast into his mouth, thrilling at the responsiveness, the faint gasp of pure pleasure. Not until he could caress the taut flesh of her belly, the gentle curve of her hip, the silky flesh of her thighs. Not until his own body was hard and throbbing with need as her hesitant fingers became bolder and bolder. Not until he could banish the last, lingering doubt about the consequences of what was happening between them and give himself over to the wild sensations that made his blood pulse with pure fire.

With one last shred of sanity, Joshua found protection and slipped it on, telling her with that instinctive, caring gesture that there would be no repeat of her past, no lingering regret for her to manage in the years to come. Whether she understood all that was beyond him. He knew only that he needed her in some elemental way that was both wonderfully simple and terrifyingly complex. Those were things he would have to sort out later, after he'd made love to her, after he'd gentled her like a skittish filly and made her his own.

Damn, he thought as he lowered himself to the bed beside her. It was going to be Garrett, after all. There didn't seem to be a damn thing he could do to stop the loving, the unexpectedly sweet emotion that crowded his heart. Not tonight. Maybe not ever.

With slow, deliberate kisses he stirred her again, his own body responding instantly, this time demanding fulfillment. Eyes locked on hers, he entered her with one slow, tormenting stroke. As her silken heat closed around him, a deep sigh of astonishing contentment shuddered through him. Then he was moving, each thrust binding them together, sealing their fate in a way that should have terrified him, but instead filled him with a sense of completeness he had never known.

Watching her, he saw the excitement build in her eyes, felt the tension in her body as it strained toward that moment of pure ecstasy that lurked again and again just beyond them. Then with one final, deep stroke, he felt her control shatter, heard her exultant cry. His own body splintered into a million sparks of dazzling light. He cried out her name and then, as they floated slowly back to reality, he murmured it again.

"Garrett, my love," he whispered with a sigh. "Oh, baby, I love you."

He felt her go absolutely still beneath him.

"What is it?" he asked at once. "What's wrong?"

Propping himself on an elbow, he studied her face, still glowing with the thrill of their lovemaking. There was no missing the troubled expression, the tiny flicker of panic that sprang to life in her eyes. Guessing at the cause, he said gently, "I do love you, you know."

"You can't," she said matter-of-factly, avoiding his gaze.

"Oh, but I can."

"You and I would be a disaster together."

"You call the last hour or so a disaster?"

She flushed. "It was a release, that's all. It could have happened between any two people who'd been through what we'd been through tonight."

"That hardly qualifies as a disaster, then, does it?" he said, barely tempering his anger.

"No, but I'd say the description fits all the other hours since you and I have known each other." She said it flatly, as if emotions could always be fit into tidy little compartments, separated as black or white. Didn't she know about the grays? Didn't she understand anything at all about the power of love?

"Okay, I'll admit we have a few little differences we'll need to work out," he conceded.

"That's like describing the Rockies as a couple of puny little hills."

"The pioneers made it across the Rockies. We can get past our differences."

Uncertainty seemed to replace rock-solid conviction. The wistful expression in her eyes made his heart ache.

"I'll prove it to you, Garrett. Give me time and I will prove it to you."

"There are not enough years in a lifetime for you to prove that to me," she said, her tone utterly bleak.

This defeated attitude threw him. Where was the woman who was certain she could conquer the world and do it alone if she had to? Or was that the problem? he thought with sudden insight. Was she convinced that she had to go it alone? He tangled his fingers in her hair and pressed kisses to her cheeks, her bare shoulders, stopping just short of the temptation of her breasts.

"Who made it impossible for you to believe in love? Was it Casey's father?"

Her eyes closed, but not before he'd seen the pain. "He didn't help," she admitted finally.

"Then who?"

"I don't want to talk about it."

"Why?"

"Because I don't like remembering."

"Sometimes that's the only way to banish the memories once and for all."

"My God, now the man thinks he's Dr. Joyce Brothers," she said with forced levity, rolling her eyes heavenward. "Where did you get your degree in psychology, Dr. Ames? Did it come with your business degree? Or was it in a cereal box?"

"Your sarcasm only proves I'm right."

Glaring at him, she jumped out of the bed and grabbed for her shirt. Holding it protectively in front of her with one hand, she reached for a blanket with the other.

"Where are you going?"

"To the sofa to sleep. It's what I should have done hours ago."

Joshua snagged a corner of the blanket and reeled her back, tumbling her down on top of him. She sat up fighting mad. "I am not sleeping in this bed with you."

His gaze pinned her. "Why not? Sleeping with me seems pretty innocuous compared with what we were doing in this bed a few minutes ago."

"A gentleman would not remind a lady of indiscretions she'd rather forget."

"I told you long ago that I'm no gentleman."

"I can see that."

Her irritation amused him. Taming her would be a delightful challenge. Capturing her heart would require all of his ingenuity and charm. Understanding her might be the most complicated—and rewarding—test of all.

With one final glare in his direction she lay down on the bed, turned her back to him and pulled the blankets up to her chin. Defiantly, Joshua lifted the blankets, fit himself to the curve of her, lowered the covers and draped an arm over her waist. He waited, then, for the inevitable explosion. Instead she merely sighed, a tiny whisper of sound that could have been resignation or exhaustion. And then she was asleep.

"Round one," he murmured victoriously, then wondered what the hell he was going to do if he actually won the fight.

Chapter Six

Garrett couldn't figure out why she couldn't move. Irritably she kicked at the blankets and felt them give, but only slightly. She tried again to roll over and realized she was pinned between the wall and some equally immovable object. A warm, breathing object. An object that seemed to draw her like a magnet.

Joshua!

Oh, Lord, she thought with a muffled moan. She really had done it this time. She had violated the single rule that had guided her life for the last thirteen years. With her hormones whizzing like an adolescent's, she had tumbled into bed with a virtual stranger. Why? Why after all this time? Why this man? It must have been the fear, the dangerous night they had survived.

Surely it had been no more than a desperate need to reaffirm life. Wasn't that exactly what she'd told him as dawn had stolen into the cabin?

Unfortunately she seemed to be the one who didn't quite buy that. Garrett knew deep inside that she had responded to some inner yearning for the promised comfort of his arms. That need she'd felt last night for the first time in years was ultimately far more dangerous than the passion. It warned her that her defenses were weak. She was not immune to Joshua's rare combination of strength and gentleness. She needed to get out of this bed, into her clothes and back to the ranch where she'd have the protection of Casey, Mrs. Mac and a dozen cowboys to keep her from making yet another dreadful, weak mistake.

She would do just that, too...in a minute. First, she wanted to take one last, lingering, intimate look at the man whose touch had filled her with life. His dark blond hair was mussed in a way that would probably have appalled his barber. The line of his jaw was shadowed with stubble, giving him a rakish, sexy look. Even in repose, his muscles were taut and well defined. The mat of hair across his chest arrowed down, narrowing to a faint line as it disappeared below the sheet that was tangled provocatively low on his hips.

Lord he was gorgeous, she thought with a sigh. She tried to drag her gaze away but couldn't. She was fascinated by the textures of his skin, by the play of light across his body. Maybe it wasn't just Joshua. Maybe she would have been equally fascinated by any masculine form. It had, after all, been a very long time since Casey's father had taken her to bed. Her eyes followed the line of Joshua's out-flung arm, ending finally at his hand, a hand that she knew from experience could caress with daring, bold strokes or tease with utmost subtlety. Just the thought of those expert touches filled her again with dangerous yearnings.

Irresistibly drawn to him, she reached out a hand, but when her fingers were no more than a hairbreadth from his chest, she jerked away. No. Maybe, if she'd been capable of viewing this as no more than a casual fling, she could indulge in one caress, but her defenses warned her against that much at least. Joshua had changed the rules by declaring his love. Such declarations weren't worth the breath wasted on them, but the temptation to believe, to trust, was always there. Garrett had learned the danger of that the hard way and it was a lesson she was never likely to forget.

Convinced that she dared stay no longer, she tried to slither through the nest of blankets toward the foot of the bed. Keeping one watchful eye on Joshua, she moved inch by inch to safety. As she crept, he turned restlessly, reaching for the space where she had been. She heard a softly muttered curse, just before she felt his fully alert gaze on her back.

"Going someplace?" he inquired, stretching lazily.

Evading his eyes, she said, "I thought I'd add some wood to the fire."

"If you'd crawl back up here, I'd keep you warm."

The seductive offer alone fulfilled that promise, she

thought as flames instantly heated her blood. "Thanks, but I think I'll stick to my original plan."

"Any special reason why you chose that particular route to leave?"

"I was hoping not to wake you."

"How thoughtful," he said skeptically, just when she was congratulating herself on her inventiveness.

Since it was too late to sneak away undetected, Garrett jumped out of bed, grabbed the clothes that had been hung in front of the fire to dry and raced for the comparative safety of the bathroom.

"Garrett," Joshua said softly just as her feet hit the icy tile.

She hesitated, her hand on the doorknob.

"I'm ninety-nine percent certain that I didn't store the wood in there."

She scowled at him and slammed the door behind her. The man was so damned smug and he had the uncanny knack of reading her thoughts, which meant it was more essential than ever that she get them off of him and back on practical matters such as getting back to the ranch, where she could put acres and acres and maybe a thousand head of cattle between them.

She stood under a steaming shower, hoping to wash away the memory of Joshua's caresses, but the slickness of the soap and water on her sensitized flesh had exactly the opposite effect. It was as if his hands were sliding over her again, reminding her, in the very core of her being, of what it meant to be a woman. She'd spent so long in what was predominantly a man's world that the rediscovery came as something of a shock. It was an awakening that could only lead to disaster, especially if she counted in any way on Joshua to keep that feeling alive on a permanent basis.

For one wistful moment she tried to imagine him staying, tried to envision a lifetime of powerful sensations such as those he'd stirred in her last night. No matter how hard she tried, though, the picture wouldn't stay in focus. He wouldn't mean to hurt her by leaving, but he would leave. There was no question in her mind about that. Getting back to what he thought of as civilization had been on his mind from the instant he'd put those fancy, impractical shoes of his into ankle-deep snow.

That meant there could be no repeat of what happened during the night—no more smooth-as-silk kisses, no more innocent touches destined to lead to something more intimate. Celibacy was something with which she'd been familiar for a long time now. There was no reason to believe she couldn't embrace that life-style again after such a brief lapse in judgment.

As Garrett brushed and braided her hair, she studied her face in the foggy bathroom mirror. Her eyes seemed wider and brighter than usual, her mouth softer and more vulnerable, her skin a healthy pink. Like a woman in love! No, more like a woman who'd lost the last of her sanity. She yanked her hair tighter, as if to tame the emotions that had caused the changes in her appearance. She stiffened her spine resolutely and curved her lips downward. Better, she decided. Unfortunately there was nothing she could do about the glow of her complexion or the defiant sparkle in her eyes.

Reminding herself that her entire future hinged on her ability to impress Joshua with her intention to pretend that nothing untoward had happened between them, she opened the bathroom door and stepped back into the cabin's main room.

While she'd been gone, Joshua had added wood to the fire. Now he was in the kitchen, humming cheerfully as he poured pancake batter onto a griddle. He glanced at her over his shoulder and smiled.

"Breakfast's almost ready. Want some coffee?"

"Sure," she said, pleased with the brisk response. Unfortunately she couldn't control her hesitant steps as well. An intuitive man would sense at once that she was running scared. As she'd already noted a dozen times in recent days, Joshua was uncannily intuitive where she was concerned.

He was also too damned attractive, she noted regretfully. With stubble darkening his cheeks, his feet bare and his flannel shirt hanging open to the waist, he promised untold masculine delights. She was caught off guard by the suggestion of intimacy that still lingered, by the captivating web of domesticity that surrounded them. She had never, in all of her adult life, shared such a morning ritual with a man, not unless breakfasts from the back of a chuckwagon during roundup counted. Not once during all of those roundups had she felt the slightest temptation to kiss the back of the cook's neck, as she did now. Drawn across the room, she was within inches of doing just that. Then she stopped, horrified by how easily her good intentions vanished in Joshua's tempting presence.

"The snow's stopped," he informed her, turning a stack of perfect, golden pancakes onto a plate and handing it to her.

She blinked in bemusement, barely grabbing the plate before it tumbled from her uncooperative fingers. "Terrific," she said aloud, but a startling shaft of disappointment speared her. If the storm had passed, it would be only a matter of time before they could return to the truck. The idea did not seem nearly as appealing as it had mere seconds earlier.

As if he'd guessed her mixed reaction, Joshua regarded her intently. "Going back won't be the end of it, you know."

"The end of what?" she said, ridiculously pleased even as she evaded his meaning.

"Us."

"There is no us," she said automatically.

"We'll see."

His tone of certainty finally snapped her back to reality. If she'd had all her wits about her, she would have smacked that smug expression from his face. Instead she hurriedly tried to inject a note of steel into her voice when she declared, "When we get back to the ranch, I expect you to steer clear of me."

"Not a chance in hell, sweetheart."

"I won't have my daughter or anyone else getting the idea that something's going on between us."

"We can always sneak out to the barn at midnight," he suggested. "Or maybe we could just steal a few kisses..."

"No barn! No kisses!" she warned him. "Or..."

A dangerous spark of defiance flashed in his eyes. "Or what?" he asked evenly.

"Or I'll have you ridden out of town on a rail," she vowed recklessly.

Joshua chuckled. "To do that, sweetheart, you'd have to tell everyone what it is I've done. You'll never do that."

She lifted her chin. "Try me."

"I already have. That's what this is all about." He straddled the chair across from her and regarded her seriously. "Garrett, I'll be the first to admit that what's happening between us is damned inconvenient. It's also probably misguided as hell. We're like oil and water, cactus and silk. But I've been around long enough to know that there's something special between us that doesn't come along all that often in a lifetime. It would be a damned shame to ignore it."

She heard the determination in his voice, but she also thought she heard a hint of wistfulness. Startled, she studied his face, trying to see some faint sign of vulnerability. If it was there, he'd covered it well. She saw only resolve in the depths of his clear gaze, stubbornness in the set of his jaw. Oddly, it was what Garrett didn't see, the longing, that terrified her the most. She could withstand Joshua's direct attacks on her senses. She could fend them off with glib sarcasm and studiously kept distance. The vulnerability, however, evaded her defenses and went straight to her heart.

Fortunately, Joshua was not a man likely to reveal his weaknesses too often. In the end, his own show of strength would be her greatest protection. Secure in that knowledge, she finished the pancakes with enthusiasm and sipped her coffee, aware that Joshua continued to watch her intently. When his attention began to unnerve her, she gathered the dirty dishes and stacked them in the sink.

"Since you fixed breakfast, I'll clean up."

"You wash. I'll dry," he countered.

"Maybe you should go shovel a path out of here for us."

Even as the words came out of her mouth, she caught him grinning at her. "Man's work and woman's work, huh?"

"Something like that," she agreed, hiding the fact that what she'd really wanted was to put distance between them. A lot of distance. It wouldn't hurt if he wore himself out, either. Then, even if they were stranded overnight again, he'd be too exhausted to want her.

"It won't work, you know."

"What won't work?"

"I'll still want you, no matter how tired I am." Chuckling at her incredulous and no doubt guilty expression, he reached for a towel. "Start washing, lady. Then we'll both go shovel the snow."

It was less than fifteen minutes before they were both

bundled up and outdoors. The stark winter landscape
had been softened by drifts of snow. The sun scattered
diamond chips of light across the endless blanket of
white. The cloudless sky was the purest azure. As beautiful as it was, though, Garrett knew the danger it represented to the cattle. They could freeze to death in a
blizzard like last night's. The hands needed to be on
the lookout for strays at once. The counterpointing of
urgent danger with the spectacular beauty of the snowfall was one of the harsh realities of life on the ranch.

"We need to get back to the truck," she said, her
sense of duty restored. "If we take the shovels along,
we should be able to dig it out of the ditch and get
back on the road."

Joshua turned her slowly until she was facing him.
With the tip of his finger, he tilted her chin until she
could no longer avoid his gaze. "Don't run away from
this, Garrett."

"I'm not running," she denied heatedly.

"You are. You've been running ever since I told you
last night that I was falling in love with you."

"What if I have? Isn't that what you're going to do?
Aren't you going to walk away from this eventually
and go back to Florida? I'm just trying to save us both
a lot of heartache."

"But you're also costing us the time it would take
to get to know each other."

"For what? So that we can be ripped apart inside a
few weeks or months from now when we finally have
to admit that we will never belong together."

"How can you predict the ending, when we haven't even begun?"

"Men like you do not end up with women like me. That's a fact, Joshua."

His jaw clenched. "What the hell is that supposed to mean? Men like me? What exactly does that mean?"

"It means that you live a certain kind of life, back in civilization, as you call it. You're rich. You can buy anything you want. Well, you can't buy me. My price tag is way too high."

Joshua ignored the rising fury in her voice. His fingers stroked her cheek, the pad of his thumb following the generous curve of her bottom lip. Despite herself, Garrett was mesmerized.

"I don't want to buy you, sweetheart," he said gently. "I just want to love you."

"No," she responded stubbornly, backing away. She had to get away from the feel of his hands on her, away from the warm glint of desire that lit his eyes and lured her like a beacon. "Absolutely not. Not again."

"You take everything too seriously," he told her, stalking her through the snow.

The sudden spark of devilment in his eyes and the lazy, flat-out amusement in his voice made Garrett very, very nervous. She held out a warning hand. "Joshua!"

"Hmm?" He stepped closer, reaching for her.

Garrett ducked under his arm and started to run, floundering through the drifts. "Stay away from me, Joshua Ames!"

"I can't," he said, gaining on her.

Garrett caught sight of him over her shoulder, turned unexpectedly and tripped him. He fell, sprawling face-down in the snow. She paused long enough to gloat, then took off, laughing at the startled expression on his face.

"Okay, that does it," he muttered, trying to keep a smile from ruining the murderous tone of his voice. "When I get my hands on you, Garrett..."

"*If* you get your hands on me," she taunted as she rounded the side of the cabin and headed for the road.

"*When,*" he repeated, gaining on her.

It was a little like being chased by the Abominable Snowman. Clumps of snow clung to his clothes and hair. He'd grabbed handfuls of the stuff, too, and was forming a gigantic snowball that she knew was destined for her. She hit the frozen creekbed running, her laughter trailing behind.

Suddenly her feet shot out from under her and she tumbled face-first into the snow on the opposite bank. Before she could even roll over, Joshua was on the ground beside her, pulling her into his arms, tumbling with her like playful kids in the season's first snowfall. The teasing attack took her back in time. Once, just once, she'd crept out of her parents' crowded, dirty apartment to see the first snowfall. Blanketed in purest white, the world for that brief, fragile moment had indeed been a wonderland, spread out before the eyes of a seven-year-old who'd seen too much of harsh reality. She had lain down on her back and made snow angels, then built a snowman, thrilling to the magical winter world she was creating. She felt the magic again now. That same innocent joy was stealing over her.

Because of Joshua. Joshua, who was trying to sneak a handful of snow down her back. Laughing, Garrett formed her own snowball, ready to retaliate. He grabbed her hand. "Oh no, you don't," he warned, his gaze locked on hers.

"No?" she questioned softly.

"No."

She let herself go limp in his embrace. "Okay," she said agreeably.

He smiled. "That's better." He shifted until he had her pinned to the ground. "Better yet," he said, his eyes blazing.

"You like this?" she inquired innocently.

"Having you under my control? Absolutely."

"There's just one thing you should remember."

"What's that?"

The hand that he'd mistakenly freed came up and jammed a fistful of snow down his shirt. As he yelped, she scooted free. "You're in the West," she reminded him sweetly. "You really should remember to watch your backside."

"And you really should watch who you challenge," he countered. He was on his feet in an instant, covering the distance she'd put between them far faster than she could increase it. Expecting to be tumbled back into the snow at any second, she gasped with shock when arms suddenly scooped her off her feet. The next thing she knew she was dangling headfirst over his shoulder.

"Joshua Ames, put me down this instant!"

"Sorry. You can't be trusted."

"And you can be?"

"Absolutely. I always do exactly what I say I'm going to do. Didn't I warn you that you couldn't run from me? Didn't I vow to stick with you like glue?"

"Where exactly are you taking me?"

"Where else? Back to my lair, so I can ravish you."

Garrett slammed a defiant fist into his back. Considering the thickness of the sheepskin coat she'd insisted he buy the previous day, the punch had no more impact than a pesky fly landing on him. Okay, she thought in resignation and an undeniable flaring of anticipation, for the moment she was going to have to concede his physical superiority. That meant relying on her wits.

The incentive was fairly powerful. If she didn't escape his clutches, she was very likely to stop listening to her head and go with her hormones, which apparently weren't the slightest bit daunted by the icy temperatures. Apparently she wasn't nearly as far removed from the cavewomen as she would have liked to believe. There seemed to be a primitive appeal to being dragged off by a chest-thumping man. There was something astonishingly heady about a man wanting her enough to make such a public declaration. She indulged in the feminine satisfaction of that for a few brief seconds before reminding herself forcefully to extricate herself from this predicament.

"Now!" she muttered aloud, in case the message wasn't getting through her hormone-induced stupor.

"Did you say something?"

"No. You know, though, since you seem to have all this energy, it would probably be a very good time for us to get to the truck. The snowplow should be along anytime. It could help dig us out."

Joshua opened the cabin door and stepped inside before he responded. Slowly he let her slide down his body until her feet reached the floor. Though he'd loosened his embrace, Garrett found she couldn't bring herself to take that one step that would have ended the contact between them. Even through the layers of clothes, her body throbbed with awareness, the tips of her breasts chafing against the warm flannel of her shirt.

"Are you so sure that's what you want?" he said softly, lowering his mouth to hers. The touch was a thrilling blend of fire and ice. He tasted of snow and to her deep regret she couldn't remember anything ever being any more delicious, any more tempting. With the tip of her tongue she tasted snowflakes as they melted on his lips, on his cheeks and finally on his forehead. Beneath her kisses, Joshua remained perfectly still, but there was a slow flaring of passion in his eyes, a faint hitch in his breathing.

Before she could stop herself, her hands came up to cup his face, her thumb imitating his earlier gesture, rubbing against his bottom lip, tracing the shape until suddenly he drew it into his mouth in one slow, utterly provoking movement that turned her insides to liquid fire.

"Damn you," she murmured as she stood on tiptoe to claim his mouth.

"I don't want this," she whispered, immediately confirming the depth of the lie by returning again and again to steal kisses that she knew would bind her to Joshua more tightly than ever.

"If you truly don't want this, stop now," Joshua warned raggedly.

"I can't," she breathed, hating the helpless rush of feelings that came over her in his arms, only in his arms.

With a groan, Joshua scooped her up again and carried her to the still-mussed bed. Hurriedly he stripped away her clothes, and then his own. As it had the night before, the fire between them raged fast and hot, consuming her with its powerful, demanding embrace. Maybe someday there would be time to linger and savor. Now there was only this violent, urgent claiming, this deep-down hunger that overwhelmed her, easing only when Joshua was buried deep inside her, when their bodies were joined in hot, elemental sex.

Shaken by the storm that swept them to the top countless times, Garrett was near tears when the sweet, devastating explosion finally rocked through her. Joshua was with her through it all, his own cry mingling with hers.

Dragging in deep, gasping breaths, she couldn't

seem to keep from whispering, "It's never been like that for me. Never."

"Not for me, either, sweetheart. Never for me, either. Now do you see why I can't let you go?"

Garrett's protest died on her lips as Joshua's arms tightened around her again. Snug against his damp chest, a deep, satisfying contentment stole over her.

Later would be time enough to let go. Later, when this wasn't so new, it would be easier to see that it could never last. Now, though, with everything in her, she wanted the feelings to go on forever.

seem to keep from whispering, "It's never been like that for me. Never."

"Not for me, either, sweetheart. Never for me, either. Now do you see why I can't let you go?"

Garrett's protest died on her lips as Joshua's arms tightened around her again. Snug against his hard chest, absorbing confirmation of his own need, Garrett would use time enough to let good sense, when this wasn't so new, would be easier to see that it could never last. Now, though, with everything in her, she wanted the feelings to go on forever.

Chapter Seven

Lying in bed with Garrett warm and yielding in his arms, Joshua was convinced he'd tasted forever and it was the sweetest, most uncomplicated thing he'd ever known. Garrett possessed strength and vulnerability in equal measure. With her unpredictable blend of serious maturity and childlike wonder, she would always continue to surprise and delight him. He needed that, responded to it in a way that was all the more remarkable because she was unlike any woman he'd ever met, yet it was as if he'd been searching for her.

Knowing how she felt, though, he was tempted to keep the two of them stranded here indefinitely, or at least until he could convince her they had a future. Though he was stunned himself that he was contemplating a lifetime commitment, he was not a man to waste time when faced with the inevitable. He wanted Garrett, needed her, and he was going to have her.

Unfortunately those happily-ever-after, forever thoughts lasted less than twenty minutes before being disrupted by the pounding on the door and a chorus of frantic shouts. Complications suddenly abounded.

"What the hell?" he said, dragging on his pants. "Who's out there? The folks who own this place?"

Garrett groaned. "No. It's Red. Mrs. Mac must have discovered we didn't stay in Cheyenne and sent him on a rescue mission. If he found the truck, he'd guess where we headed."

Joshua had his doubts about Mrs. Mac being behind Red's untimely arrival. From the speculative gleam he'd seen more than once in Mrs. Mac's canny eyes, he guessed she'd leave them right where they were. He wasn't quite so sure about the ranch foreman. On the few occasions when they'd crossed paths, he'd suspected Red had his own plans for Garrett. He'd probably initiated this rescue attempt all on his own.

"Mom?" Casey yelled just then. "Mom, are you in there?"

"Oh, dear Lord," Garrett moaned, turning dismayed eyes on Joshua.

He squeezed her hand. "It's okay. I'll go out. You get dressed."

"But she'll know," she said, yanking on a shirt and fumbling with the buttons as she leapt out of the bed.

Joshua put his hands on her shoulders and regarded

her intently. "Slow down, sweetheart. Maybe, *maybe,* she'll guess. She won't *know.* And even if she does, would that be so horrible?"

Garrett broke free and began snatching up sheets and clothes that had been scattered every which way. "How can I teach her about morals and being responsible, when I go and do something like this?"

Joshua removed the pile of laundry from her arms and tossed it on the sofa. "There's nothing more moral than love. I love you."

"You do not," she countered furiously. "Joshua, could we debate this some other time? It sounds as if they're about to break the door down."

"I'll take care of it. Just settle down and get dressed."

He noticed with regret that his promise didn't wipe the worried expression from Garrett's face. They really were going to have to work on the trust angle, he thought as he swung open the door and stepped outside, pulling on his jacket.

"Hey, angel," he greeted Casey, warming at the smile that instantly spread across her face. "What are you doing here?"

"You're okay," she said, flinging her arms around him with obvious relief. "Is Mom inside? Is she okay, too?"

"Everybody's fine. She's getting dressed," he said, turning his gaze on Red, who was regarding him warily.

"I think I'll just check on her," Red muttered, stepping toward the door.

Joshua's hand gripped his arm. He could feel the tension that spread through Red's body and prayed the man wouldn't decide to turn their test of wills into a brawl. "I said she was getting dressed," he said quietly. "She'll be out in a minute."

"And I said I want to check on her," Red repeated, his jaw clenched, his massive shoulders squared. The glint in his eyes seemed to take Joshua's measure. Under other circumstances Joshua might have been willing to give him the fight he obviously craved. It would have settled things between them once and for all.

Casey seemed to pick up on the faintly antagonistic byplay between the two men at once. "Is something wrong?"

"Nothing, angel," Joshua told her, returning Red's fierce gaze and daring him to hint otherwise.

Red's body finally relaxed, but the protective gleam in his eyes didn't dim. "I'm sure your momma's fine, honey. I was just gonna see for myself, but I guess there's no need if she's on her way out."

Casey seemed to accept the explanation. She faced Joshua. "We found the truck in the ditch. Did you run it off the road? Mrs. Mac said you probably weren't used to driving in the snow."

"Danged fool thing, trying to drive in that blizzard," Red said accusingly. "Could have gotten the two of you killed. You'd think even a greenhorn would know better."

"Actually, Garrett was driving when the truck went off the road. Another driver nearly skidded into us and she had to swerve to avoid him."

The knowledge that it was Garrett who'd crashed the truck didn't seem to temper Red's irritation. "Still say you didn't have any business being on the road in the first place. Should have stayed in Cheyenne."

"You're probably right about that," Joshua agreed, though he wouldn't have traded the past twenty-four hours for anything in his previous experience. "The storm turned bad before we realized it."

Just then the door opened again and Garrett stepped out, a forced smile on her face. There were lines of strain across her brow. Joshua wished he could wipe them away, but he knew she would evade his touch.

Garrett opened her arms and Casey ran into them. Her eyes met Red's, then darted nervously away. Joshua nearly groaned. If the foreman had any doubts at all about what had been going on inside the cabin, her skittish demeanor would confirm his suspicions. Garrett's attempts to struggle for an air of nonchalance were downright pitiful. In a perverse way Joshua was almost pleased. It meant she'd had few, if any, previous occasions calling for subterfuge.

"I see the cavalry has arrived," she said too heartily. "Thanks, guys. How'd you know to come looking for us?"

"I got worried, Mom. Mrs. Mac said you were okay. She said you'd probably decided to stay in Cheyenne, but I called the hotel where you always stay anyway.

They said you never checked in. I told Red and we came looking. We found the truck. Red says you're lucky you didn't break your 'danged necks,'" she added, obviously quoting the man precisely.

Red had too many *danged* opinions, as near as Joshua could tell. He scowled at the man, who was eyeing Garrett as if she were a plate of chow after a long day on the range.

With her hands poked into the back pockets of her jeans, Garrett was suddenly all business. The transformation was uncanny and a little irritating. Joshua wasn't quite sure what he'd expected when they first confronted the outside world again, but it wasn't this quick shedding of the vulnerability that had touched him.

"Red, are the men out checking on the cattle?" she asked when Joshua wanted her to go on being just a little flustered, just a little pink-cheeked with embarrassment.

"Went out at first light."

"Any problems?"

"None I'd heard about by the time we left our trucks back a piece. The hands have been in touch on the CB. No need to worry yourself. I've been through more of these blizzards than I care to recall. I know what to do."

"Of course, you do. It's just that..."

She turned toward Joshua. Before she'd even completed the sentence, he shrugged in resignation. "Go on back. I know you have work to do. I'll get back to the truck and bring it home.''

"We can stop and tow it before we go back," Red offered grudgingly. "I'll leave it down by the creek."

"That'll be fine," Joshua told him, avoiding Garrett's gaze. "I'll clean things up inside before I go."

"I'll help," Casey offered. "I don't need to get back right away, do I, Mom? I can make sure Joshua finds the truck okay."

Garrett appeared reluctant, but she said only, "Are your chores done?"

Casey nodded. "There was no school, so I did 'em this morning. I even baked cookies with Elena until I got really worried about whether you were stranded someplace. I guess it's good that I worried, huh?"

Garrett's eyes met Joshua's for no more than a second before she nodded and said, "Yes, real good, sweetheart."

"Can I stay?"

"If Joshua doesn't mind."

"No, I'll be glad of the company, in fact." Even if it was the wrong company. Maybe he could use the opportunity to pry some information from Casey that would help him in his campaign to woo her mother.

He refused to be caught staring wistfully after Garrett as she left with Red, so he turned and headed back inside.

"Joshua."

Garrett's voice halted him. He looked back at her. "Bring the laundry on back to the house, okay?"

He nodded and closed the door. Casey was standing in the middle of the floor, studying the room curiously. "There's only one bed," she announced.

"Yep, that's right."

"Does the sofa open up?"

"No, it doesn't. Why the fascination with the sleeping arrangements?"

"Well, you and Mom were here alone all night. I mean, what did you do?"

"We played cards."

"I meant about sleeping."

He could feel a brick-red blush creeping up his neck. "I slept on the sofa," he claimed, thankful that the sheets had been dumped on top of it to lend a certain credence to the statement.

Casey regarded him disbelievingly. "You're too tall." Her gaze narrowed. "Did you and Mom sleep together?"

"Sleep together?" he repeated in a choked voice.

"You know, did you have sex?"

How in hell did anyone ever raise a teenage daughter? he wondered weakly. Struggling for composure, he asked, "Don't you think that's a rather impertinent question?"

Casey grinned. "Mrs. Mac says I'm precocious."

"Well, Mrs. Mac is right. Did she also mention that it's a trait you might want to keep in check?"

"I guess that means you did," she said, losing him completely.

"Did what?"

"Sleep with Mom."

"I never said that."

"When people don't answer you directly, it generally means they think you won't like the answer or that you're not grown-up enough to hear it."

Joshua caught himself grinning and carefully wiped the smile from his lips before he faced her. "And just where did you pick up that bit of insight into human nature?"

"Mrs. Mac and Mom. They never answer my questions."

"Maybe it's because you ask the wrong ones."

"You mean because they're personal."

"Exactly."

"But this one's not really personal," she said earnestly. "I mean, don't you think it affects me, too, if you're going to get involved with my mom? I mean, you could end up being my dad or something."

Sensing a mine field, he asked carefully, "And how would you feel about that?"

Casey looked thoughtful. "I guess it would be okay, as long as you didn't tell me what to do and stuff."

"Then we have a problem, young lady, because I most definitely would be inclined to tell you what to do."

She turned startled eyes on him. "You would?"

"Absolutely. I may not be up on the rules of parenting, but I think that's what dads do, even stepdads."

He couldn't mistake the flaring of hope in her eyes. "Does that mean you're really going to marry Mom?"

Joshua decided that Garrett would not appreciate learning of their impending engagement from her daughter. "Bundle those sheets and towels up in a pillowcase. It'll make them easier to carry."

"I guess that means you are," Casey said, grinning. "Great. I'd almost given up on her, you know."

"Given up?"

"On getting Mom to get married. Mrs. Mac had, too," she confided.

"Don't count your chickens before they're hatched."

She looked puzzled for an instant, then nodded. "You want me to keep my mouth shut until you can convince Mom."

He nodded. "It might be wise."

"You're probably right. She always hates it when I figure things out before she does."

"I'll bet she does," Joshua said with a laugh. "I'll just bet she does."

By the time they had straightened up the cabin and made their way to the truck, which Red had left on the side of the road near the frozen creek, it was already nearing dusk again. Joshua cast one last look in the direction of the cabin, aware that the last twenty-four hours had changed his life. If only Garrett would admit to the same thing, he thought. Instead he kept visualizing her going off with Red the first chance she got.

"What does your mom think of Red?" he asked Casey as they started home.

"She likes him, I guess." She regarded him closely,

her eyes widening in sudden understanding. "Oh, you mean, like does she think of him as a boyfriend or something?"

Joshua winced. "Yes," he admitted reluctantly.

"Nah. She's known him forever and ever. He helped her get the job at the ranch. I think maybe he used to go in the diner where she was working when she first got here. He likes her a lot, but Mom's pretty picky. She doesn't date a lot."

"I'd think she'd be asked out all the time."

"Oh, she is, but she won't go unless Mrs. Mac puts up a fuss. Mom says there's no point in wasting her time and their money. She said she made up her mind a long time ago that she'd never get married. Why do you suppose that is?"

"Hey, kiddo, you're the one with all the answers."

"Well, it could be because she never got over my dad. She never talks about him or anything. I used to ask, when I was little, but she'd get all sad, so I finally stopped." Suddenly her expression turned wistful. "I wish I knew something about him. It's weird not knowing."

Joshua felt as if someone had sucker punched him. He'd sensed the hurt that Casey kept well-hidden behind her facade of precociousness, but it had never occurred to him that Garrett might still be carrying a torch for the man who'd fathered Casey, then left her alone. For all their sakes, he resolved to get some answers the minute he could get Garrett alone.

Unfortunately, Garrett seemed to have some very set

ideas about handling what had happened between them in that cabin. Within minutes of his arrival back at the ranch, he could tell she planned to ignore it—and him.

It was another twenty-four irritating, thoroughly frustrating hours before he was finally able to corner her in the barn, where she was rubbing down a beautiful roan horse that looked far too big and feisty for her. He had visions of that wild-eyed beast spooking and taking off, tossing Garrett and leaving her lying injured in the snow.

The horse sensed his presence before Garrett did and began prancing restlessly in its stall. When the horse tossed it's head, ripping the reins from Garrett's hand, she said quietly, "Joshua, I think you'd better leave." She still hadn't turned around.

Joshua chuckled despite himself. "How'd you know it was me?"

"I know the effect you have on women," she retorted. "Apparently that extends to Bright Lightning here, too."

Bright Lightning? Good Lord! Couldn't she ride a horse named Old Dobbin or something? He knew better than to suggest it. He settled for saying, "My male ego tells me to take that as a compliment, but I have a hunch you didn't mean it that way."

She shrugged. "Take it however you like."

He edged toward the stall, where the horse was finally beginning to quiet down. Reaching into his pocket, he took out a sugar cube and held it in the palm of his hand. The huge roan whinnied in delight and took it, then nudged his shoulder for more. Garrett shook her head. "Tamed another one," she said dryly.

Joshua stayed silent, rationing out sugar cubes, while Garrett continued to curry the horse. When both were calmer, he said, "I'm not trying to tame you, Garrett."

"Aren't you?"

"Of course not. Your spirit is what makes you who you are."

"You know nothing about my spirit, Joshua. You know next to nothing about me."

"I know that your skin feels like satin." His voice dropped seductively. He tipped her chin up so he could look into her eyes. "I know that your eyes turn midnight blue when I make love to you. I know that your hair is the color of sunlight, that you can beat the daylights out of me at poker, that you have a hearty appetite..." His eyes locked on hers as he added, "For everything."

An unmistakable shudder swept through her and she closed her eyes to hide the fiery sparks that had turned them the rarest shade of sapphire. When she blinked them open an instant later, the heat in their depths had chilled. "That's only a part of me."

"A part you've ignored for far too long."

"Don't you think you're being a little presumptuous?"

"Maybe," he replied noncommittally, bunching his hands into fists at the possibility he might be wrong. "But I don't think so."

"Okay, let's say for the moment that you're right.

Let's say that I'm some love-starved cowgirl, stuck out here in the middle of nowhere. What makes you think I want anything more from you than a quick roll in the hay?'' Flashing eyes echoed the challenge in her voice.

Joshua flinched at the crude statement. ''If all you wanted was temporary gratification of your sexual urges, you could have turned to Red or any of the other men who no doubt lust after you all the time.''

''But you're so much more convenient. You'll be leaving. There won't be any messy sentiment, no lingering complications involved.''

''Just love,'' he said softly.

Her voice climbed. ''You do *not* love me!''

Bright Lightning whinnied nervously.

''I'll prove it, if you'll let me.''

Only a man as determined and intuitive as Joshua would have caught the wistfulness that swept over her face for no longer than a heartbeat. ''No,'' she said firmly.

''Coward.''

She whirled on him then. ''I will not be some damned experiment for you, Joshua Ames. You can't goad me back into your arms.''

''I will do anything I have to to get you back in my arms.'' He stepped closer and again lifted her chin with his finger. His voice dropped. ''Consider it fair warning, Garrett. I will do *anything*.''

He could feel her trembling, could tell that she was torn between fury and longing. As he anticipated, she went with the anger, aiming her open hand straight at his cheek. He caught it in mid-swing. Keeping his gaze on hers, he kissed the palm of her hand, swirling his tongue over the faintly callused flesh until he could hear her breathing quicken in the hushed air.

"Remember this, too," he warned. "There's nothing I like more than a good fight."

The sneaky, low-down devil! The minute Joshua left her alone, Garrett turned the barnyard air blue with her opinion of him. Most of the obscenities ranked him somewhat lower than a snake's belly or took a stab at defining his parentage. She was pleased with the increasing range of her expletives, until she heard his laughter ringing out on the winter wind. The creep had heard every word. Worse, he found her outburst amusing. The patronizing son-of-a...

"Mom!"

She swallowed the rest of her diatribe. "In here, Casey."

Dressed in jeans that were frayed at the knees and a jacket that was exactly like Garrett's, Casey looked like an active, happy teenager. Garrett studied the glow on her cheeks and the sparks in her eyes and reminded herself that this was what her entire life had been about. All she wanted was for Casey to grow up surrounded by love and fresh air and an appreciation for hard work. She wanted Casey to take for granted the independence that her mother had had to fight so hard to attain. She wanted her to be strong enough to withstand whatever knocks came her way.

Casey swung herself up onto a saddle that was sitting astride a sawhorse. "How come you were using all those words you won't let me say? Are you mad at Joshua?"

"Yes," she said, knowing it would be useless to deny what Casey had already heard with her own ears.

"How come? I think he really likes you, Mom."

"I don't think so."

"But he told me..." she began, then choked off the rest of the sentence.

Garrett's gaze shot to her flustered daughter. "Told you what?"

"Nothing."

"Casey, don't lie to me."

"But I promised, Mom. You wouldn't want me to go back on my word, would you?"

Actually she would, but she knew she couldn't ask it. "No," she said wearily. "What do you want for dinner tonight?"

"Pizza," Casey said at once. "You've been promising and promising. Will you make it tonight?"

"How about you making it? We have all the ingredients."

"Sure. Is it okay if I ask Joshua?"

"No!"

Expecting Casey to protest the terse response, Garrett was startled to see that she was grinning. "I guess you're really mad at him, huh?"

"Look, sweetheart, I don't expect you to understand, but this is between Joshua and me."

"Grown-up stuff, huh?" Her grin broadened. "Great!"

"Great?"

"Yeah. He must be making progress."

"Progress?" Garrett repeated weakly.

Casey dismounted and ran for the door. "Gotta go, Mom. I'll have the pizza ready in a half hour. Don't be late."

"Hey, who's the mother here?"

"Sometimes I think it'd be better if I were," Casey said, a mischievous glint in her eyes. "Then you'd listen to my advice."

Garrett chuckled. "When I want your advice, short stuff, I'll ask for it."

"I guess I shouldn't hold my breath."

"Probably not. Now go. I'm starved."

Dead tired and fueled by irritation, Garrett finally got back to the house an hour later. "Sorry I'm late," she called out as she dropped her coat over the back of a chair and headed toward the kitchen. The inviting scent of garlic filled the air, along with Casey's laughter. Since her daughter had become addicted to the telephone and boys almost simultaneously with her thirteenth birthday, she thought nothing of it. She tugged off her boots and padded toward the kitchen in her stockinged feet.

She had one foot through the doorway when she realized that Casey was sitting at the table and the phone was in its cradle. The hairs on the back of her neck rose.

"Hi, sweetheart," Joshua said cheerfully. "We saved you some pizza."

Garrett turned furious eyes on her daughter, but Casey ignored the glare. With a wink at Joshua, she stood up and headed for the door.

"See you guys later," the little traitor announced. "I have homework."

"You didn't even have school today," Garrett said, desperate to keep her from leaving. "Stay and have a soda with us."

Casey and Joshua exchanged a glance that was all too knowing.

"It's a report," Casey said. "It's due next week. I think it's going to take a lot of time, way more than I thought."

"Thanks for keeping me company, kiddo," Joshua said. "The pizza was great."

"Thanks. See you later."

Then she was gone and there was no place for Garrett to hide.

Chapter Eight

"What are you doing here?" Garrett demanded, her fingers clenching the back of a chair. Deep inside she was aware of a brief flash of jealousy. Joshua and Casey were so comfortable together. An instantaneous bond had sprung up between them that somehow made her feel left out. She wanted to be a part of that easy camaraderie, even as she distrusted it.

Furious at the contradictory feelings raging inside her and blaming Joshua, she glared at him as she waited for an answer he seemed in no hurry to give. The kitchen, normally cozy and warm, suddenly felt stifling. With Casey's departure, she felt abandoned, left to face the danger of Joshua alone. The charged atmosphere pulsed with tension. She wanted to sit down, but knew that the minute she did she'd be giving him an edge, admitting to her nervousness.

"I just came calling, ma'am." One of his most beguiling smiles spread across his face.

Garrett's heart thundered. Her gaze narrowed. "Don't try some *aw shucks* routine on me. Didn't you hear a word I said to you earlier?"

His irritating grin broadened. "Quite a few words, as a matter of fact. Be thankful it wasn't Mrs. Mac who heard you. She'd be washing your mouth out with soap."

Garrett's lips twitched with impossible-to-contain mirth. "She probably would," she admitted ruefully, then stiffened as she recognized how close the conversation was to veering off into something perfectly civil. She had no intention of being polite to a man who'd invaded her privacy, who'd plunked himself in the middle of her home when he knew very well that she didn't want him there.

"Let's stick to the point," she said. "You and I both know that Mrs. Mac has nothing to do with this."

"Sorry. I didn't mean to distract you."

"You didn't."

"Oh, really," he said softly, his eyes gently accusing her of the lie.

Garrett's gaze slid away, evading. "Damn it, Joshua, don't you take anything seriously?"

"I take you very seriously."

"Don't start with that again. Just tell me how you finagled your way in here."

"I knocked."

"Simple as that, huh?"

"Casey has very good manners."

"I don't suppose she invited you in the first place."

"Why? Did you tell her not to?"

Garrett flushed.

"I see that you did," he said wryly. "Oh, well, I won't take it personally."

"You should." Her expression sobered. "I don't want you here, Joshua. Not in my home."

"Because I represent a threat."

"Yes."

"To what?"

"To my life-style, my peace of mind."

His brows rose a fraction. "Just by stopping in to bring you a bouquet of flowers."

"Flowers?" she said blankly as he gestured toward the kitchen counter. An old-fashioned cranberry glass pitcher was filled with a huge, colorful assortment of fragile spring blossoms. Deeply touched and unwilling to admit it, Garrett's breath clogged her throat. She blinked against the damnable sting of tears. She wanted to touch them, to get close enough to smell the sweet aroma. Because Joshua was in her way, she didn't. She held her distance.

"Where on earth did you find them?" she inquired, carefully tempering her enthusiasm.

"I didn't go out and pick them, if that's what you were wondering."

Garrett couldn't take her eyes off of the blooms. No

one except Casey had ever given her flowers and that was hardly the same. Casey's ragged bouquets of smushed wildflowers had been presented by grubby little hands. This array looked as if Joshua had plundered a vivid spring garden. No florist in Cheyenne could have come up with this spectacular, unseasonal arrangement. She lifted her gaze to his. "Where?" she repeated.

"I had them flown in."

"Flown in?"

He shrugged. "Even though you seem to think it's a crime, being rich does have some advantages."

Garrett's pleasure dimmed perceptibly. The casual explanation robbed the gesture of something that a moment before had seemed so special. The flowers, the extra effort, meant nothing to a man like Joshua. He could have imported the entire orchid population of Hawaii, if he'd been so inclined. It was probably part of his regular seduction timetable, listed on some computer index along with his appointments and handled by an efficient secretary. In her case, the romantic gesture had come after the fact, but he struck her as a man who would veer only so far from his routine.

"They're very nice," she said flatly.

She saw the faint puzzlement creep into Joshua's eyes, the quick flare of anger. "What's wrong?"

"Nothing. They're lovely. Thank you."

"Enough of the polite good manners. What the hell's wrong now? Two minutes ago you looked as if I'd presented you with diamonds. All of a sudden it's as if they've turned into garden worms or something. Is it what I said about being rich?''

Before she could form a denial, he shook his head. "That's it, isn't it? What the hell is wrong with having money?''

"Stop cursing.''

"Why? I'm not using any words you haven't flung about today.''

"Lower your voice. Casey will hear you.''

"Don't you want her to know what a stubborn, pig-headed woman she's got for a mother?''

Garrett sighed regretfully. "I'm sure she's already aware of that.''

"Well, it can't be my language. She's sure as hell heard worse.''

"Joshua!''

He leaned forward intently. "Talk to me, Garrett. Tell me what's wrong with having money.''

She dragged her fingers through her hair, tugging strands loose. He was pushing her back to that *other* time again, forcing memories she didn't want to face. "It's not the money exactly.''

Joshua refused to settle for the weak evasion. "Then what? It's legal. I don't pedal drugs or export arms to the enemy, so what's the problem? Talk to me, Garrett. We need to get past this.''

"We don't need to do anything. I'm sure you earn your money perfectly legitimately. I'm sure you're wallowing in it. I just don't want any part of it.''

He leaned toward her until his hot, angry breath whispered across her cheek. "Why, Garrett?"

Something finally snapped in her. "It's what you do with it, okay? What all men with money do."

His eyes turned suddenly cold. "Let's leave other men out of this for the moment," he suggested, his tone frosty. "What precisely do I do with my money that you find so offensive?"

Memories flooded in, crowding out the image of the man across from her and replacing it with the man she hated, the man she despised. Tears streamed down her cheeks as she accused him, "You use it to control people, to buy and sell them, to get your own way no matter the cost."

As if it came from far away, she heard Joshua's sharp, furious intake of breath. Dragging herself back to the present, to this moment and this man, she watched with a sinking sense of dismay as his shoulders tensed and a dull red color crept into his cheeks.

"When did you come up with this particular insight into my personality?" he said tensely. "Was it the flowers? Forget the damned flowers."

With one violent sweep of his arm, he reached back and knocked them off the counter, sending them crashing to the floor. Pink and apricot tulips and bright yellow daffodils mixed with shards of cranberry glass and water. Holding back a gasp, Garrett had to resist the desire to reach out and rescue the precious, broken blossoms.

"Maybe it was earlier," he accused. "Maybe it was the minute I arrived here eighteen months ago."

Garrett winced in guilt.

He sighed sorrowfully. "I'm right, then. You made up your mind about me way back then and nothing— not even making love with me—nothing that's happened since has done anything to change it. Do you know how pathetic that is? Are you going to spend the rest of your life shutting people out based on some crazy first impression of how they squander their bank account?"

"No. Yes." Her own fury kicked in then, renewed by his derision. "Yes, I am. If that's what it takes to keep us safe, that is exactly what I'm going to do."

"Safe?" Joshua asked, his expression suddenly troubled. "What is that supposed to mean? I'm no threat to you."

She shook her head wearily. "Yes, you are."

"I think you'd better explain."

"I can't." She looked up, wiping furiously at her tears. "I just can't."

She heard his sigh of defeat, knew precisely when he got to his feet. Her breath held, her heart aching, she waited for him to leave. Finally, to her astonishment, he leaned down and kissed the top of her head.

"You may be stubborn and pigheaded, Traci Maureen Garrett, but so am I," he said softly. "So am I."

The walk back to the house cooled some of Joshua's anger. For a full minute in that kitchen he'd wanted to shake Garrett until her teeth rattled for making such horrible judgments about him. The tears had held him back, shaken him in fact. With a sudden flash of insight he'd known with absolute certainty that her response was based on the past, not the present. Her own past. It had nothing to do with him at all. If he was going to understand her, he had to find out what had happened to her years ago to rob her of her ability to trust. Unless he could do that, he might as well return to Florida and forget all about her.

He went back into the main house through the kitchen and found Elena polishing the silver.

She looked up at his entrance and smiled. "Señor Ames. You missed dinner. Are you hungry? I could make you something. There are enchiladas."

"Thanks, Elena, but I ate with Casey."

"Ah," she said, beaming. "And Garrett, *si?*"

"Afraid not."

"She was still working? It is too late. She works too hard, that one."

"Yes, she does." Picking up a rag and a beautiful silver coffee carafe, he began to polish. The mindless task soothed him, giving him pleasure as he watched the soft sheen replace the tarnish. Was that what it would take with Garrett, a gentle touch to wipe away years of built-up hurt?

"Were you here when she first came, Elena?"

The housekeeper gave him a sharp look. "*Si*, I was here. The *niña* was just a baby. They came here from the hospital."

"Did Garrett ever talk about the baby's father?"

Mrs. Mac stepped into the kitchen just in time to hear the question. "If you want to know something about Garrett's past, don't you think you ought to be asking her?"

Joshua wasn't fazed by the rebuke. "Every time I broach the subject, she shuts up like a clam. Even Casey hasn't been able to get anything out of her."

Mrs. Mac looked startled. "The child told you that?"

He nodded, his expression grim. "She finally stopped asking. It can't be healthy for either one of them to keep this veil of silence thrown over the past."

"No," Mrs. Mac agreed slowly. "I've suspected for some time that there was more to the story than Garrett has ever revealed to me."

"What has she told you?"

Mrs. Mac looked troubled. "Joshua, I understand your need to know, perhaps even better than you do yourself."

"I love her, if that's what you mean."

Elena burst into excited Spanish, kissing him on both cheeks. Mrs. Mac nodded thoughtfully. "You surprise me."

"Didn't think I was capable of love, huh?"

Something that might have been a smile tugged at her normally stern lips. "No, young man. I wasn't sure you had the guts to admit it."

"I don't like to waste a lot of time and energy ignoring the inevitable. I'm going to win her over, Mrs. McDonald. Will you help me?''

''Yes,'' she said without hesitation. ''I think our Garrett has finally met someone worthy of all she has to offer and man enough to make her see it. It could take time, though. Promise me you won't give up on her. It could be a bumpy ride.''

He grinned. ''She warned me of exactly the same thing, only in a slightly different context. I don't scare easily. I guess if I did, I'd never have made the trip out here, no matter what Cal did to persuade me. Something told me eighteen months ago I was lost when it came to Garrett. I managed to persuade myself that the feelings would diminish with time and distance and sanity, but they haven't,'' he concluded with a shrug. ''I guess the only thing left is to come up with a battle plan.''

''I can see to it that the two of you are thrown together,'' Mrs. Mac offered, her eyes snapping with excitement at the prospect of matchmaking. ''We could have a party. This old house hasn't seen a wonderful, romantic ball in many years.''

''The party might be good, but forget the rest. I think Garrett's had her fill of being maneuvered. What she may have missed is a simple, old-fashioned courtship.'' A chagrined expression crossed his face. ''Come to think of it, so have I. This could be fun.'' He met Mrs. Mac's sparkling gaze. ''Any suggestions? What worked on you? I heard you were a softie when it came to ice-skating. I'm not sure I have the ankles for that, but I could try."

A dreamy look came into her eyes. "So Garrett told you about that, did she? Skating under a full moon certainly sets the right mood for romance. In the meantime, though, you could start with flowers, lots and lots of flowers."

Joshua threw back his head and laughed. "I've already tried that one. They wound up on the kitchen floor."

Suddenly the memory of the scene just a short time before came back to him.

"Of course, I was the one who put them there," he admitted thoughtfully.

Before he'd sent them crashing, before the fight had erupted, he'd seen the wistfulness in Garrett's expression, seen the shimmering tears of delight in her eyes before the gift had been somehow spoiled. Maybe what she needed rather than lavish bouquets was one single rose.

Chapter Nine

Garrett found the single, perfect rose lying on her saddle when she went to the barn at dawn a few days after her fight with Joshua. She'd been so successful in avoiding him that she'd actually convinced herself he'd given up on her. Soon he would finish his work and return to Florida where he belonged. Now with the sweet scent of the white bud counterpointing the more familiar earthy aroma of hay and horseflesh, she realized he had only been giving her room to breathe.

"Oh, Joshua," she murmured as she touched a finger to the velvety softness of the petals. The man was definitely sneaky, sliding through her defenses just when she thought she was immune to his charms. Anger had been her best defense so far, but how could she possibly get angry over something as beautiful and unexpected as this?

The barn door squeaked on its hinges just then and she looked up, fully expecting to find Joshua. Her traitorous pulse hammered at the prospect. Filled with a mixture of anticipation and dread, she slowly turned, only to find Red stomping his boots on the ground and shaking the snow from his jacket. Deep inside her, relief warred with disappointment.

"You riding out with us today?" he asked when he saw that she was saddling Bright Lightning.

"I thought I would."

He nodded, his expression turning thoughtful. Garrett recognized the look. He was worried. Instantly she was all business.

"Red, is something bothering you? Is there something happening around here that I should know about?"

He glanced pointedly at the rose. "You tell me."

"Meaning?"

"You've been jumpy as a June bug these last few days. You're standing here clutching a rose and now you want to take off to check the fence in the northwest section. I'm just trying to figure if any of that has anything to do with what's going on between you and this Ames fellow."

"There is nothing going on between me and Joshua. Nothing," she said too quickly, too emphatically. Her gaze skidded guiltily away from his, then determinedly returned to see Red's eyes narrow consideringly.

"Well, now, I might have believed that if I hadn't seen the two of you coming out of that cabin the other day. The tension was thicker than a morning fog in the Tetons. Just now you jumped about a foot in the air when I opened that door. Unless I miss my guess, you was expecting him."

She shook her head. "Not really."

"Hoping for him, then."

"Absolutely not."

Again he nodded slowly. Garrett was busy congratulating herself on the success of her deception when he said, "Maybe, just maybe, you can fool yourself, woman, but you can't fool me. I've known you too long. I've seen the way you keep a man at arm's length and do it with a smile, so's he never knows he's been flat-out rejected. Lord knows, you've done it enough to me and the other cowboys around these parts. If you'd been shut up in that cabin with any one of us overnight, you'd have walked out of there in the morning just as cool as you pleased. Instead your face was all flushed like you'd been riding lickety-split over the back forty."

Garrett felt a renewed blush creeping into her cheeks. "Red, this really isn't any of your business," she reminded him.

"Maybe. Maybe not. But I know what I saw. If the man did a thing to hurt you, I'd expect you to tell me about it. I'd take care of him so he wouldn't bother you again. You and Casey are pretty special to me and to all the men. Either of you ever need anything, all you have to do is ask."

The sweet satisfaction of being cared for brought fresh tears to her eyes. "Thanks. I know I can count on all of you, but there's nothing to worry about. I'm a grown woman. I can handle Joshua."

"If you say so," he said doubtfully. "He the one who gave you that flower?"

"Yes."

"Means a lot, a man giving a woman a flower like that, wouldn't you say?" Red commented shrewdly.

She thought of all the flowers Joshua had delivered to her house a few nights before and the way they'd ended up all over the kitchen floor. "It's just a rose."

"You ever found one waiting for you out here in the barn before?"

"No."

"Then I got one last thing to say and I'll stay out of it till you come askin' for advice. You watch your step around a man like that. You ain't used to his slick, big-city techniques. Before you know it a man like that'll have you all mixed up, doing something you're likely to regret. You'll wind up getting hurt. None of us around here wants to see that."

Garrett sighed. She knew more than Red could ever imagine about slick, big-city techniques and a whole lot about regrets. She recognized a practiced seduction technique when she saw it and certainly knew better than to believe that a single rose meant anything. Regretfully she let the flower slide from her fingers and drop to the barn floor, its significance as faded as its petals were likely to become.

"Let's get going," she told Red, taking Bright Lightning's reins and following the still-troubled foreman outside. Ominous gray clouds scudded by overhead. As she closed the barn door she glanced inside and saw that the rose had been trampled. Blinking back tears, she mounted her horse and turned toward the north, into the cold that suddenly seemed crueler than ever.

Joshua found the crushed rose late that afternoon. A swift fury swept through him, followed by a growing sense of resignation. This wasn't going to follow the quick battle plan he'd envisioned. Winning Garrett was obviously going to require an all-out campaign. Maybe he could get Mrs. McDonald to speed up plans for the ball. He very much needed to hold Garrett in his arms again and he doubted she'd let him do it except on a dance floor.

He went back to the main house and found Mrs. McDonald in the parlor going over the books he'd just finished working on. "Checking to see if my addition's okay?" he inquired.

"Looking to see what you've embezzled," she taunted right back. Shrewd blue eyes assessed his mood and her tone softened. "Did you find Garrett?"

He didn't even bother to ask how she'd known that's where he'd gone. "No. There's no sign of her."

"It's my guess that she rode out with Red and the men. There have been problems with the fencing."

"Is that part of her job?"

"No, but she likes to ride when she's thinking about something. My hunch is that you've given her a lot to think about the past few days."

The thought of her out there with Red grated on his nerves. For the first time in his life he was afflicted with a nasty streak of pure jealousy. "Any idea which direction they were heading?"

"I know exactly."

He glanced at her and found that her gaze was studiously fixed on the columns of figures in front of her. "Would you care to share that information with me?"

"No."

"I thought you told me you were going to help me."

"That's what I'm doing. Chasing after her like a man who has the right to won't win her over." She looked up at him then. "Don't threaten her independence, Joshua. She'll only come to resent you."

He sighed as he recognized the wisdom in her advice. "What should I do, then?" he said, wandering around the room, picking things up and putting them down.

"Wait and while you're at it, you might take a look at my personal checkbook. It doesn't seem to match the statement I got last month from the bank. Hasn't for some time now," she added.

"How do you expect to find signs of embezzlement,

if you can't even balance your own account?" he teased.

"Gut instinct, boy. Don't you dismiss that so easily."

"I wouldn't dream of it."

"Joshua, seriously, if you're starting to get restless here already, maybe Garrett's not the woman for you."

"Meaning you don't think she'll ever be a whither-thou-goest sort of wife."

"Precisely. She went through a lot to get to Wyoming in the first place and as far as I can see, it's given her something she very much needed. She'll fight to keep it."

Suddenly he was afflicted with the unexpected and confusing sense that he was in a situation in which he was absolutely helpless. He didn't like not being in control. He hated the uncertainty. "Why does love have to be so damned complicated?" he growled, thumping an original Remington bronze back onto its pedestal.

"It's not the loving that's complicated," Mrs. Mac told him. "It's the details. If you think of it that way, the two of you should be able to work out anything. Now I think I'll go take my nap."

"If you can rest easily that must mean the books are okay."

"So far," she retorted. "So far."

She struggled to her feet. Holding herself erect, despite the pain that was reflected in her eyes, she crossed the room and patted his hand. "Use this time that Garrett's away to think things over carefully. Don't start something that you can't live with. It wouldn't be fair to either one of you.''

"I'm not sure how much thinking I'll be able to get done between now and dinner,'' he told her. "It could take me longer than that just to decipher what you've scribbled in this checkbook.''

"There's no rush. Garrett's not likely to be back tonight. Chances are they won't make it back for a day or two, especially if we get another snowfall tonight.''

Joshua's eyes widened and thoughts of his own snowbound night with Garrett sent a dozen provocative memories racing through his mind. "A day or two,'' he repeated, more disgruntled than ever. "I'm supposed to relax while she's out on the range for a day or two with a bunch of cowboys?''

"If you can't do it now, it won't get any easier,'' Mrs. Mac warned him. "That's just something more for you to think about.''

"Well, hell,'' he muttered when she'd left the room.

"I heard that,'' she called back.

Chuckling ruefully, he shouted, "Sorry.''

When she'd gone, he continued to prowl the cluttered room restlessly, unable to rid himself of the image of Garrett riding off with Red. Again. Once more she'd chosen the company of the ranch foreman over him. Maybe it was a losing battle after all. He allowed himself ten minutes of thoroughly dispirited thinking, then snapped himself out of it. He picked up the phone and started making calls.

By the time Mrs. Mac came down to dinner, he'd had a fax machine and his own phone line installed. In the morning some of his most critical files would arrive by overnight express. If he was going to stay here and fight for Garrett, then he might as well stay busy. It was entirely possible that three-fourths of his jealousy problem resulted from not having enough to occupy his own time.

Mrs. Mac took in the new equipment and nodded in satisfaction. "Settling in, I see."

"I hope you don't mind."

She grinned at him. "Not a bit. I was worried you might leave. I take it this means you won't."

"Not until she orders me away."

"I thought she had."

"Okay, not until she really means it."

Mrs. Mac chuckled. "That's the spirit," she said, thumping her cane on the floor in approval. "Why don't you go over and get Casey? I expect she's doing her homework so she can play chess with you tonight. She'd probably like to help us plan that party, too. I think it's time we got busy on that, don't you?"

"Absolutely."

"Then get a move on, boy. These things don't just happen, you know."

When Joshua went outside he was surprised to discover that the night had turned foggy as a warm front moved in to push away the Arctic air of the previous days. Instead of more snow, it seemed they were in for a bit of Indian summer. Fortunately he had a solid sense of direction. He made it to Garrett's house with only one slight detour into the side of a truck.

Still rubbing his bumped shin, he tapped on the door. "Casey, it's Joshua. Mrs. Mac says dinner's almost ready."

The door opened wide and Casey greeted him with a grin. "Hi. I'll be ready in a minute. I'm having trouble with my math."

"Bring your books along. Maybe I can help you with that after dinner."

"That would be great. Then we can play chess, okay? I was reading the book of rules you gave me today."

"When did you have time to do that?"

"In study hall."

"Maybe you should have been doing your math then."

"Why, when I knew you could help me tonight?" she said, tugging on her jacket and gathering up a stack of books.

"What if I'd said no?"

"You wouldn't," she said confidently. "You're trying to get on Mom's good side."

He certainly couldn't fault her logic, except for one tiny thing. "Your mother isn't so crazy about the idea of you and me spending time together."

"That's just what she says," she said dismissively. "Don't you know anything about women?"

"Apparently not. Would you care to enlighten me?"

"Well, I probably don't know about all women, but

I sure know Mom. She, like, says a lot of stuff she doesn't really mean, when it comes to men."

"Why would she do that?"

"I figure it's because she's scared. If she chases them away, then she can keep things just the way they are."

"And how do you feel about that? Are things okay the way they are?"

Casey's hesitation and the brief sadness that flickered in her eyes were answer enough. "Sure," she answered loyally.

"Really?" he pressed.

"Well, they're okay for me, I guess, but I'm pretty nearly grown up. I won't be around here forever. What'll happen to Mom then? I mean, sometimes I think she gets pretty lonely now. She doesn't say anything. It's just the way she looks." She stared up at him hopefully. "She hasn't looked that way as much since you came. Now she just looks scared."

"And that's better?"

She seemed to puzzle over her answer before finally saying, "I think so. Don't you?"

"I think we'll just have to wait and see."

She snuck her hand into his and held on tight. Joshua wasn't exactly sure who was reassuring whom.

During dinner Joshua was struck by the sense of family that crept over him. Here he was with a woman who wasn't his own grandmother and a teenager who wasn't his own daughter, yet he felt a contentment he hadn't felt in years. If only Garrett were at the table with them, he was certain he would feel complete.

His own childhood had taught him the value of family and the warmth that came from shared meals like this. His mother had been the kind of woman who'd insisted that everyone be at the dinner table at the same time night after night. It had been the one time of the day set aside for catching up on everything from schoolwork to international politics. Even when he'd been sick, she had seen to it that he came to the table. On the rare occasions when he hadn't been able to, she had insisted that the family gather in his room so he wouldn't feel left out of the warmth and camaraderie. Tonight he realized how much he'd missed it.

That realization also gave him his first clue about why his relationship with other women had never felt right. Most of them had had active careers of their own. Dinners had been catch-as-catch-can affairs, sometimes coming at midnight and consisting of Chinese take-out. Maybe he was more old-fashioned than he'd ever realized. He really enjoyed long, lingering conversations over a home-cooked meal. The affectionate bantering between Mrs. Mac and Casey amused him and in no time at all the two of them had drawn him into it.

"Okay, you two, uncle. It's not fair ganging up on me," he accused.

"Sure it is," Casey protested. "You just have to fight back."

He rolled his eyes. "Whatever happened to showing respect for your elders?"

Mrs. Mac waved a finger at him. "That's the last thing I expected to hear from you, young man. You haven't given me a shred of respect since the day you arrived."

"Deep down I respect you," he countered.

Chuckling, she retorted, "Maybe you could get it to the surface a little more often."

"I'll work on it," he promised. "Now what about this party? How can I help?"

Casey's eyes lit up. "We're having a party?"

"I thought we might," Mrs. Mac said. "Let's get Elena in here and talk about food."

"Can I invite my friends?" Casey asked.

"I don't see why not. That's the fun of a party around here, seeing all the generations together under one roof."

"Will there be square dancing? I went to the party over at Rutgers's last year and they had square dancing. It was fun."

Joshua groaned as he saw his plans to hold Garrett close vanishing in a flurry of whirling and bowing. "I was kind of looking forward to an old-fashioned waltz," he muttered.

Mrs. Mac's eyes sparkled with mischief. "The last dance at my parties is always a waltz."

"The last dance," he repeated weakly. How the hell would he ever make it through an entire evening without taking Garrett into his arms? How would he be able to bear watching her with men like Red, who were bound to be more adept at the lively square dances he'd never tried?

"Seems to me there's something to be said for anticipation," Mrs. Mac said.

"If I anticipate any more, it'll make me crazy," he said just as the door leading to the kitchen burst open. He took one look at Red's anxious expression and his heart plummeted.

"Where's Garrett?" he said at once, his voice barely under control and only because he didn't want to upset Mrs. Mac and Casey.

"There's been an accident," Red said, meeting his gaze head-on.

"Where the hell is she?" Joshua repeated, gritting his teeth together to keep from hurling accusations in the foreman's face.

"At the hospital. She's fine, really. It's just a broken ankle."

"Sit down," Mrs. Mac ordered, casting a warning look at Joshua. She shouted for Elena. "Bring Red some coffee and a plate." She turned back to the man who was sitting uneasily on the edge of his chair, warily watching Joshua. "Now tell us what happened."

"Her horse stumbled. Must've been a hole under the snow. Won't be able to tell for sure till the snow melts. Anyway, she was thrown. The snow cushioned her fall, but her ankle got caught in the stirrup. That's what did it, I suspect. She's got a few other bruises and a scratch or two, but she'll be out in the morning, according to the doc. He put a walking cast on, but said she ought to stay off her feet as much as possible. He warned her if she didn't, he might have to put on a hip-high cast and keep her on crutches. You should have heard her when he suggested that.'' He shook his head. ''Didn't know she knew that many ways to cuss a man out.''

Casey was listening, her eyes wide. ''I want to see her.''

''No need for that, honey,'' Red said. ''There's no need to be driving in this fog. You call her on the phone if you want. She'll be home first thing in the morning. I'll get her myself.''

Joshua saw the worried look in Casey's eyes and was certain it reflected his own. Deep in his gut he was convinced that Red was telling them everything, that if Garrett was blistering the air, she would be just fine. Even so, he knew he'd never rest until he'd seen her for himself.

''I'll take you,'' he told Casey.

''Let the woman get her rest,'' Red argued, but fell silent at Joshua's fierce expression.

''Come on, Casey. Get your coat.''

The drive to the hospital was the longest of his life, made worse by the thick blanket of fog that was every bit as treacherous as Red had suggested. Casey kept her eyes open for landmarks and was every bit as responsible for their safe arrival as he was.

''Thanks,'' she said to him when they finally reached the door to Garrett's room. ''Thanks for bringing me.''

''I wanted to be here, too, sweetheart. Just remember, if your mother's asleep, don't wake her.''

Casey nodded and pushed the door open, then tip-toed in. Joshua stepped inside behind her. Garrett was lying on her back, her eyes closed, her hair spread across the pillow. With her cheeks almost as pale as the crisp white sheets, she looked beautiful and vulnerable. There was a faint scratch across her forehead and a bruise that shadowed the tender skin along the inside of her elbow. A white-hot rage churned inside of Joshua and he wanted to take Red and the horse responsible apart, bit by irresponsible bit.

Garrett's left leg, with its cast up to her knee, was propped on top of a pillow. She had balled a fistful of blanket into one hand and tugged it up under her chin, like a child might hold a security blanket.

Casey went to the chair beside the bed and sat down, her shoulders finally relaxing as she reached for her mother's free hand. Joshua pulled a second chair up beside her.

"They've probably given her something to make her sleep," he told Casey.

"That's okay. I just want to be here. Mom's never been hurt before." She turned a beseeching look on him and for the first time since he'd met her, he could see the little girl's uncertainty that she usually kept well hidden. "We can stay, can't we? I mean until morning, in case she wakes up. We'd be here to take her home, then."

He reached over and squeezed her shoulder. "I wouldn't want to be anyplace else, sweetheart. Of course, we'll stay."

With a sigh, Casey inched her chair closer to his and leaned against him. Before he knew it, she was asleep, still clinging to Garrett's hand. He put his own hand over theirs and whispered a prayer of thanks that Garrett's injuries hadn't been worse.

For hours he sat without moving, his eyes on Garrett, watching the soft rise and fall of her chest, listening for any hint that she might be in pain, damning Red for letting this happen to her. Over and over he warned himself to hold his temper once she woke. She wouldn't appreciate his accusations, nor would she take kindly to any of his protective instincts.

Joshua knew from his own experience that hovering over Garrett would only be interpreted as an attempt to break her spirit. He'd felt the same about his mother's smothering concern more than once, even though rationally he'd known she was only worried about him. Now he began to see how difficult it was to allow someone he loved to have the freedom to take risks. The true depth of love was letting go. It had always seemed so simple to him, but it wasn't, not when it filled his heart with this terrible, aching fear.

Maybe loving Garrett was going to teach him a thing or two about his own past, he decided as he drifted to sleep. Maybe she wasn't the only one with something to learn about love.

Chapter Ten

Garrett woke up feeling grumpy and sore as hell. Her mouth was dry. Her shoulders and back ached from slamming into the ground and from sleeping in the same uncomfortable position all night. Her ankle was throbbing and her ego was seriously bruised. Of all the idiotic, stupid things to happen. She was an experienced rider. Losing her seat when Bright Lightning stumbled and getting tangled in that stirrup had been silly, greenhorn mistakes. She'd be lucky if any of the men ever showed her a lick of respect again.

She sighed deeply, indulging herself in a rare bout of self-pity. When tears threatened, she blinked them back and determinedly dragged herself back to the present. Berating herself now wasn't going to accomplish anything. The accident had happened. She ought to count her blessings that the injuries weren't worse. If Red hadn't chased down Bright Lightning and reined her in, they would have been. Once more, she owed him. A tear trickled down her cheek. She really hated owing anyone.

Enough, she told herself sternly. If she kept this up another five minutes, she'd wind up crying her eyes out. She'd be better off trying to figure out how the devil she was going to manage a ranch if she couldn't even get on a horse for the next few weeks. Not that Red couldn't be trusted to do whatever needed to be done with the cattle. He'd been doing that long before she came on the scene. She was supposed to spend her time making management decisions. It was essentially an office job. She was the one who'd chosen to make it into something more. She was the one who'd insisted on riding out to see for herself what was happening, on working the roundups and the brandings, on surveying the fence lines and watching over repairs.

When she'd first arrived, she'd been expected to handle little more than the most basic record keeping and supply orders, but filled with hope and ambition, she had wanted to learn everything. Mrs. Mac had encouraged her. Garrett suspected she had reminded Mrs. Mac of her own early initiation into ranching. She had been generous in sharing her knowledge. Over the years they had come to work well together, even more so since Garrett had become Mrs. Mac's eyes and ears, doing all of the physically exhaustive tasks that the old woman had once relished doing herself. Garrett sighed at the prospect of giving all of that up, even for a short time.

"So, sleeping beauty, you're finally awake."

Startled by the low, husky voice, she turned her head and looked straight into Joshua's anxious eyes. She could read the exhaustion on his face, see it in the slump of his shoulders. Even so, his gaze caressed her and her breath caught in her throat. Despite all of her best intentions, she was very glad to see him. For an instant she was tempted to reach out to him, to draw on his strength and the comfort she knew he would offer all too willingly. Then she saw Casey sound asleep in the chair next to him and remembered the danger he represented.

"What on earth are you doing here?" she whispered, her tone guarded.

"Casey was worried about you." He reached for her hand and she felt his concern steal into her heart. It would be so easy, she thought, so easy to let this man into her life, to let him take care of her. He could give her everything she'd ever dreamed of.

He could also take it all away, leaving her far worse off than she was now.

"You scared the dickens out of me, too," he admitted, not taking his eyes off of her until he had looked her over from head to toe.

"I'm okay," she offered shakily. Afraid of the feelings that he aroused in her, she tried to pull away, but he only held tighter, then pressed his lips to her knuckles. The tenderness in his eyes, in his touch, tugged at her, made her long for all the things that they'd shared that one precious night, things that could never be again.

"You look like you've gone a couple of rounds with a nasty coyote," he observed.

She winced. She must look ten times worse than that for him to say it at all. "I think he won. Don't worry, though. I'm made of sturdy stuff. I'll just be a little wobbly for a while. How long have you been here?"

"Since last night."

"Last night? Why didn't you wake me?"

"You were dead to the world. You needed the rest."

"I'm sure I'm going to get more rest than I ever wanted over the next couple of days," she said wryly.

"Weeks," Joshua corrected with a smile that didn't quite reach his eyes.

"Days," she argued stubbornly. She caught her breath as she tried to shift her leg to a more comfortable position.

"Pain?" he said at once.

"A little."

"Which means it's just this side of unbearable, I suppose."

She grinned weakly. "Something like that."

"I'll get the nurse."

"Don't move," she ordered, gesturing toward Casey, who had shifted until she was leaning against him. "I'll ring for her. What time is it?"

"Barely six. You should try to get some more sleep."

"What about you? That can't be comfortable."

"The last time you said something like that, we ended up in the same bed." His gaze fell on the hospital bed. "It's possible, I suppose."

Her pulse lurched all too hopefully, but she shot an alarmed look at her daughter. "Joshua, Casey is..."

"Sound asleep. I'll stop teasing, though. Do you need anything besides the painkiller? Something to drink, maybe?"

"A toothbrush."

"I doubt the gift shop is open yet, but let me go check around." He squeezed her hand again and settled Casey more comfortably. "I'll hurry that nurse up, too."

"Thanks."

As soon as he left the room, Garrett saw Casey's eyes blink open. She suspected her daughter had been conveniently playing possum.

"Hi, Mom. You feel okay?" she inquired with a yawn.

"Probably better than you do after spending the night on that chair. You should be at home in your own bed. You have school today."

"If you hadn't gone and done something dumb like this, I would have been home."

As always, Garrett found herself grinning at her daughter's fascinating mental gymnastics. "So, it's my fault," she concluded.

"You've got to admit that what you did was pretty silly. Weren't you concentrating or something?"

"I guess not."

"Were you thinking about Joshua?"

Since that was exactly what she'd been doing, Garrett could feel herself blushing. "Where would you get an idea like that?"

"Mom, it's not exactly a secret that you like him."

"Oh, really?" Oh, Lord. Why couldn't she have had a teenager who was oblivious to everything except clothes and boys? This was not a conversation she wanted to have with her daughter.

"Mom!"

"Okay, yes. I like him. Joshua is a very nice man." Her tone sobered and she forced herself to say something she probably should have said the minute she'd seen the bond beginning to form between Joshua and her daughter. "Honey, Joshua is only here for a short time. It wouldn't be wise for either one of us to count on him too much."

"He'd stay if you asked him to."

If only that were true, she thought wistfully. "No," she said firmly, the denial meant as much for herself as for Casey. "His life is in Florida. Please, sweetheart, don't get too close to him. He'll go away and I wouldn't want you to be disappointed when that happens."

"Joshua won't leave us," Casey protested, her expression turning mutinous. Garrett could tell she was shaken and for a minute she almost hated Joshua for coming into their lives and disrupting things. She'd wanted so badly to protect Casey from life's hurts, from the anguish of being left behind. Now it seemed inevitable that they were both in for heartache. She reached for Casey's hand.

"He will have to go back sooner or later," she said gently. "And that's okay. We're lucky to have known him as a friend."

"Mom, he wants to be more than our friend. I know it."

"Honey, even with the best intentions things don't always work out."

"But I know you love him, Mom. And he loves you."

The certainty in Casey's voice startled her. "Has he said that?"

"No. I mean, not exactly. Mom, I just know, okay."

"There are different kinds of love, sweetheart. Whatever Joshua said, I'm sure he meant it at the time, but there are things that just aren't meant to be," she explained flatly.

"But Mom..." Casey protested.

Garrett winced against the pain. "Honey, that's enough. I don't want to discuss it anymore right now."

Casey opened her mouth to argue, but Joshua came back to the room just then, a nurse with him. By the time Garrett had been given a shot for the pain and had brushed her teeth, Casey had fallen completely silent. Garrett caught the suddenly distrustful look her daughter cast at Joshua and sighed with regret. In the long run, though, it was better that Casey not count on anything permanent. She had to learn that the only person a woman could ever really count on was herself.

Joshua couldn't imagine what had happened during the short time he'd been gone from the room. Casey's mouth had turned down into a frown and she refused to meet his eyes. Garrett looked miserable and he suspected it had nothing to do with the pain since the shot she'd been given should have kicked in by now.

"What's up?" he asked cautiously. "You two have an argument?"

"No," they answered simultaneously, not looking at each other or at him.

"Then let's cheer up a little. I ran into the doctor out there and he said he's springing you, as long as you promise to follow orders. I told him that Casey and I would chain you down if we had to."

"That won't be necessary," Garrett mumbled. "One stupid mistake is all I can handle. I'll do whatever he thinks is best."

Joshua regarded her doubtfully. "That'll be a first. Casey brought you some clean clothes last night. I'll wait outside while you get ready to go."

Garrett nodded.

"Casey, you want to wait with me?"

She glanced at him, then just as quickly looked away. "Mom might need me."

He nodded. "I'll be waiting just outside, then."

In the hallway he tried to figure out why the tension

in the room had suddenly been as thick as last night's
fog. Maybe it had something to do with the fact that
Casey had spent the night at the hospital, maybe Garrett was angry because Casey was going to miss school
today. That would have been an easy enough explanation, but Joshua couldn't quite buy it. He'd seen the
bleak expression in Casey's eyes. He'd noticed how
she seemed to avoid meeting his gaze. Unless he
missed his guess, they had argued about him.

When the door finally opened and Garrett hobbled
out, she allowed him to take her arm. She protested
only mildly over having to leave in a wheelchair. She
thanked the nurses. She thanked the doctor. She even
thanked him for being there to take her home. In fact,
she was altogether too agreeable. She kept up a cheerful, nonstop monologue all the way to the car. The
change in the weather seemed to fascinate her. She
commented on it endlessly.

But all of Garrett's talking couldn't cover Casey's
unnatural silence. He knew teenagers were prone to
sulking, but he'd never seen any signs of it in Casey.

"Want to stop for breakfast?" he suggested as they
drove out of the parking lot.

"I'm starved," Garrett admitted. Casey said nothing.

"Any suggestions?"

"We could stop at Frank and Lena's diner, where I
used to work. I haven't seen them in ages."

"Is that okay with you, Casey?" He glanced in the
rearview mirror and saw rather than heard her mumbled

response. He nodded. "Okay, then. You point the way."

Garrett guided him onto the highway, then to a turn-off just out of town. The diner, which was essentially a double trailer, sat by the side of the road, its red neon sign flashing hopefully against the gray sky. A handful of pick-ups lingered in the parking lot. Joshua pulled into the spot closest to the front door.

"You stay right where you are," he warned Garrett. "I'll get you."

"Joshua, I can walk a few feet."

"And get your cast soaked in the snow. Not a chance." He reached in and scooped her up before she could rally another protest. "Casey, lock up for me, okay?"

She regarded him sullenly, but did as he'd asked. Joshua opened the door to the diner and was instantly assailed by the aroma of fresh-baked muffins, bacon and coffee. A tall, lean woman wearing an apron glanced up from the grill and let out a whoop that was part joy and part dismay.

"Traci Maureen Garrett, what have you gone and done to yourself?" she clucked, rounding the counter to help with Garrett's coat.

"I took a spill from a horse," Garrett said.

"Well now, honey, that doesn't sound a bit like you," she said, regarding Garrett with concern, then turning to Casey and wrapping her in a hug. "Now, let me just look at you. I swear you've grown another five inches since the last time you and your mama were in here. Pretty soon you're going to be taller than your mama and twice as pretty.''

Casey's mouth curved into a hesitant smile that faded almost before it began. She slid into the booth next to her mother, as if to protect her from Joshua.

Lena turned to him. ''Now, just who are you, handsome? I don't recall seeing you around here before and I know all the good-looking cowboys. Can't say I blame Garrett for keeping you all to herself.''

Joshua held out his hand. ''Joshua Ames. I'm doing some work for Mrs. McDonald.''

''Of course. You're that bookkeeper from back east.''

He grinned ruefully. ''Not exactly, but that's close enough.''

''Well, I'm mighty glad to know you. Now what can I get you all to eat? Casey, honey, you want your French toast like always?''

''I guess,'' Casey mumbled.

Lena shot a penetrating look at her. ''Then why don't you give me a hand over here. You always were a better cook than your mama. How about you, Garrett? Scrambled eggs and bacon?''

''Perfect. Potatoes and biscuits, too. I'm famished.''

''And I suppose you want the works, too?'' she said to Joshua. ''Eggs sunny-side up?''

''How'd you know?''

''Lucky guess,'' she said with a wink. ''I'll be right back with the coffee.''

When Lena went back behind the counter, Casey

went with her, clearly anxious for the escape. When she didn't return with the food, but remained with Lena, Joshua frowned. "What's up with Casey?"

Garrett looked momentarily guilty, then lifted innocent eyes to challenge him. "Nothing."

"Garrett, the girl hasn't said two words in the last hour. Now maybe for some kids that would be normal, but not for Casey. She's usually chattering a mile a minute."

"It's probably just a delayed reaction to the accident and seeing me in the hospital."

"Maybe," he said doubtfully. "I'll talk to her when we get back to the ranch."

For an instant, a look that might have been fear flashed in Garrett's eyes before she looked down at her eggs. "Leave her alone, Joshua. It's just the way teenage girls are, up one minute and down the next."

"Have you talked to her about what's bothering her?"

"Joshua, she is fine," she insisted, but he noticed that she suddenly seemed to have lost her appetite. She was pushing her eggs around on her plate and when she finally tired of that, she went to work on her toast, breaking it into inedible little pieces.

"What did you say to her?" he asked finally.

Her gaze shot up, met his, then skidded away.

"That's it, isn't it? You had a fight."

"Okay, yes. But I'm telling you it was just one of those mother-daughter things."

She might have been convincing, if her hands hadn't been trembling so badly.

"Did my name come up in this mother-daughter talk?"

"Joshua, not everything revolves around you."

"I'm well aware of that, but you'll have to pardon me for seeing two and two and coming up with four. It's the mathematician in me."

"Well, this time you've totalled wrong."

"You won't mind if I ask her that, will you?"

Her cheeks flooded with scarlet. "Yes, damn it. This is none of your business."

"It is if it involves me."

"You keep saying that and you have absolutely nothing to go on."

"I have the fact that Casey and I have grown very close since I came back to Wyoming. She has confided in me. As recently as last night, she seemed to trust me. Now she won't even look me in the eye. You add it up."

He could see that his words had hit the mark when her shoulders drooped and the color drained from her face. "Please leave it alone," she begged softly.

"I wish I could," he said with a deep sigh. "But I love the two of you every bit as much as if you were already my family."

He was ready to say more, but she cut him off. "We're not your family."

"Not yet."

"Not ever."

Suddenly he realized the toll the argument was taking on her. Her eyes were shadowed with fatigue. "Look, this isn't something we're likely to settle now. We'll discuss it later."

"There's nothing to discuss."

"You are an incredibly repetitive woman."

"And you are an exhaustingly stubborn man."

"An interesting match, don't you think?"

"Joshua!"

"Let's go get you into bed, sweetheart."

"In your dreams."

His eyes widened with feigned innocence. "What a wicked mind you have, my dear."

"Oh, go to hell," she muttered, but there wasn't much spunk behind it.

"Whatever you want," he said agreeably.

She glared at him.

"Ready to leave?"

"Do I have a choice?"

"Always. I can sit here sipping coffee all day long, if that's your preference."

"Then I'd like to go home, Joshua."

"I do so love it when you're docile."

"If I weren't loaded up with pain medication and immobilized by this cast, I'd show you just how far from docile I'm feeling right now," she informed him, her eyes flashing.

He grinned. "I'll take a rain check."

Her lips twitched and, though she fought it admirably, laughter bubbled out. "Oh, Joshua," she said with a sigh. "You are impossible."

"No, sweetheart, I am very possible." He dropped a kiss on her nose, then another on her lips. He might have lingered there for an eternity, tasting the sweetness, memorizing the shape, savoring the warmth, but Casey chose just that moment to join them.

Avoiding Joshua's eyes, she said stiffly, "I want to go home now."

"Your mother's tired, too. If you'll get her coat, we'll hit the road."

For an instant he thought she might not go. She cast a reluctant look toward her mother, but she went. Joshua figured he had just enough time for one last kiss, but Garrett thwarted that by hobbling away to say goodbye to Lena. Chagrined, he went after her. When he slid her coat around her shoulders, he leaned down to whisper in her ear, "Later."

She never once missed a beat in her conversation with Lena, but he felt the shudder that swept through her body. It wasn't much for an impatient man, but it was the most he was likely to get. It would hold him... for a time.

Chapter Eleven

Garrett was a lousy patient. She had the temperament of a bear with a thorn stuck in its paw. Joshua had the devil's own time trying to get her to let him take care of her.

Over Garrett's strenuous objections, Mrs. Mac had insisted on settling her into the main house so that she could be properly looked after. The room she'd chosen, with a definite twinkle in her eyes, happened to be just down the hall from Joshua's. Garrett had warily gauged the distance, then retreated into silence.

Once left alone, she had stayed dutifully in bed for about two minutes. She had been halfway down the stairs when he'd caught her, scooped her up and carried her back. An hour later when he'd taken her a bowl of vegetable soup for lunch, she'd practically flung it in his face. Then she'd ordered him out of her room, out of the state, out of her life. She'd emphasized it by pointing the way.

Joshua crept back an hour later and found her asleep. He lingered in the doorway, unable to take his eyes off of her. The sight of her in that bed, even clad in a less than provocative nightshirt, did amazing things to his pulse. Guiltily—the woman was in pain, after all—he backed out the door. He was about to close it when her eyes blinked open. She sat bolt upright, stared around in momentary confusion, then sagged slowly back to the pillow.

"Feeling any better?" he asked, stepping inside but keeping a careful distance between himself and that all-too-tempting bed.

She groaned and turned her back on him. "Go away."

"Can I get you anything?"

"My files," she said, turning a hopeful look on him.

"How about a magazine?"

The counter offer drew a fierce scowl. "I have work to do. I want my files."

"How about a stockman's journal?" he compromised. "It wouldn't be my choice of leisure reading, but you might like it."

"I want my files."

"You have a decidedly one-track mind."

"So do you but I get paid for mine."

"You're on vacation."

"I don't take vacations."

"You do now."

"Says who?"

Mrs. Mac stuck her head in. "Says me. How are you?"

"I broke my ankle. That's hardly cause for all this fussing," she grumbled.

Mrs. Mac approached the bed far more bravely than Joshua dared. She plumped the pillows, ignoring Garrett's sour expression. "Maybe it's about time you let the rest of us fuss over you. You work too hard. The ranch won't collapse if you take some time off."

Joshua could tell from the suddenly fearful look in Garrett's eyes that Mrs. Mac's reassurance had exactly the opposite effect. "Just think what fun you'll have catching up," he taunted her. "Hours and hours of work piled up. You'll be able to feel incredibly noble."

Mrs. Mac regarded him oddly, then caught on. "That's right. The work will be waiting. I don't know of anybody here who's likely to snatch it out from under you and see that it gets done. Now why don't you pretty yourself up a little and let Joshua carry you downstairs for dinner. I brought you a lovely new robe." She handed over some pink satin and French lace confection that set Joshua's pulse racing.

Fingering the satin cautiously, as if she feared the very femininity it suggested, Garrett said, "I can get down the stairs on my own."

"And spoil my fun?" he protested. "Not on your life. Need any help getting dressed?"

She shot an appealing look at Mrs. Mac, who was chuckling. She scowled. "Traitor."

Mrs. Mac drew herself up to her full, imposing height. "Humph! Some people don't see what's staring them right in the face."

"Which is? I'm sure you'll be happy to point it out to me."

Mrs. Mac shook her head. "Actually, I won't. I think I'll leave that to Joshua. Dinner is in forty-five minutes. If you'd like a glass of sherry, you'll need to hurry."

"From the look of things, I could use the whole damned bottle," she muttered, but she swung her legs over the side of the bed and hobbled into the bathroom. When Joshua repeated his offer of help, she slammed the door.

"Guess not," he said, and stood back to wait for her.

It was a pattern that was repeated for the next three days. Garrett's mood deteriorated with each passing day that she was confined to her room. She snapped at Elena. She had Casey fleeing the room in tears. Even Mrs. Mac was giving her wide berth by the end of the third day. Only Joshua dared to venture into the room. He waved a white handkerchief first, then poked his head in.

"Don't shoot. I'm unarmed."

"Unfortunately so am I." She was sitting in bed, her arms folded across her chest, glowering at him.

"You have a nasty attitude."

"It's not getting any better being cooped up in here."

"Then I think I may have just the thing. Put on your warmest duds, sweet thing. I have a surprise for you."

Instantly her eyes flared with more excitement than she'd demonstrated since he'd made passionate love to her in that cabin. "You're taking me home?"

"Better than that."

"There isn't anything better than that."

"See if you still feel that way in an hour. Now, speed it up before I change my mind."

"Five minutes," she vowed. "Don't leave me."

His expression suddenly sobered. "Never. Haven't you figured that out yet?"

Garrett sank back on the bed in defeat. There was no way in hell to get her jeans on over that damned cast. And if she couldn't even get dressed, how could she go with Joshua? It was a measure of her boredom that she couldn't bear the possibility of missing this outing. Emotional dangers and pitfalls were the least of her worries. The unceasing sameness of these last few supposedly relaxing days was about to drive her out of her mind. She would have made a bargain with Satan himself to escape this tedium. Joshua pretty much fit into the same category.

She tugged on her jeans again, but they were hung up on that cast and no amount of coaxing was likely to solve the problem. She needed scissors.

"Joshua!"

He opened the door a crack. "Ready?"

"I need scissors."

His glance fell to the jeans that were sagging around her right ankle. Slowly his gaze worked its way from bare ankle to calf, from calf to dangerously exposed thigh. He swallowed hard as his gaze settled on the scrap of lace masquerading as panties.

"Scissors?" he repeated in a choked voice.

"My jeans won't fit over the cast."

"So I see." Laughing eyes that still smoldered with desire met hers. "Maybe I can help."

Now it was her breath that was snagging. "Scissors would be better," she said, but he was already kneeling in front of her, his fingers hot against her bare skin as he caught the cuff of denim and ripped. He tore it very, very slowly, his gaze studiously on the task, his fingers sliding along her leg. The feathery caress was sheer torment.

"Is that far enough?" he finally asked.

Tongue-tied, Garrett nodded, then glanced down. "There's just one thing," she said, unexpected laughter suddenly threading through her voice.

Joshua's dazed eyes met hers. "Hmm?"

"It's the wrong leg."

His glance shot to the jeans. As he took in the ripped right leg and the cast on her left leg, he rubbed his hand over his eyes. "It's your fault. When I touch you, I can't concentrate."

"Then don't touch me," she said.

"I can't do that, either," he warned, sounding helpless for the first time since she'd met him. His hands rested on the bed on either side of her hips. She sensed the turmoil raging inside him as he kept his hands away from her. With her own heart pounding, she knew she had to find some quick way to break the spell that was slowly weaving its way around them.

"Then at least do me one favor, okay?" she said, tangling her fingers in his hair.

"Anything."

"Stay away from the rest of my wardrobe."

She counted the heartbeats before Joshua finally chuckled and the tension snapped.

"Good idea," he agreed briskly. "Now do you have anything else to put on that doesn't require alterations or should I finish off these jeans?"

"I suppose you'd better finish them off. Maybe we can stop by my house for some more clothes while we're out."

Joshua draped a blanket around her this time, while he opened the left seam from ankle to knee.

"Try these," he said, handing them to her and scurrying for the door. If she hadn't known exactly how he felt, Garrett might have laughed at him. Unfortunately her own pulse continued bucking like a bronco.

Her heartbeat took another lurch when she saw Joshua's surprise waiting on the front lawn. An old-fashioned sleigh, sleek and black, the bright red reins dotted with silver bells, sat in the front yard. Two horses pranced in place.

"A sleigh ride," she said, her voice filled with wonder. "Where on earth did you find it?"

"Mrs. Mac thought she remembered it being in one of the outbuildings. There was a dust cover over it and boxes piled on top. The runners were rusty. I've been polishing the sleigh up the last three days. Do you like it?"

"I love it, but you hate being out in weather like this. Are you sure you want to do this?"

"Do you?"

"Oh, yes," she breathed.

Joshua smiled. "Then I'll love it."

He lifted her up and placed her carefully on the seat, then climbed up beside her. Red plaid blankets were quickly tucked around their legs. "All set? Is your leg comfortable? I put some pillows down so you could prop it up."

She reached over and impulsively kissed him. "You're wonderful."

"I keep telling you that," he said, but she could tell that he was pleased. Just for today, for these next couple of hours, she vowed to relax and say only what was in her heart. Somehow she would find a way later to live with the consequences.

Joshua snapped the reins and the tinkling sound of the bells rang out as the horses took off at a sedate clip. The sleigh glided across the snow, giving her an entirely new perspective. This was familiar territory zipping past, starkly beautiful in its own way. She had always loved it for the freedom and independence of spirit it represented, but today through fresh eyes, she viewed it as a place of romantic enchantment, as well. Icicles glistened on tree branches. The air was crisp again, the sky cloudless.

Eventually they stopped and Joshua poured steaming hot chocolate from a thermos into huge mugs, added a dollop of brandy and plopped a handful of marshmallows on top. Garrett took the first sip. "Delicious."

"Not half as delicious as you," he murmured, his gaze locked on her lips. "Your mouth is covered with chocolate and you have this tiny bit of marshmallow."

"Where?" She reached up with a napkin, but he brushed her hand away.

"Let me." His tongue slowly ran around the outline of her mouth, tasting, until Garrett was sure that the bottom would drop straight out of her stomach. There it was again, that strange, wonderful warmth that Joshua was able to generate deep inside of her. It was better than a bonfire. Snuggled cozily in his embrace, she felt a rare contentment steal over her.

She sighed. It was only the faintest of sounds, but it immediately drew a worried frown from Joshua.

"You okay?"

"Never better." She slid her hand into his. "How can I ever thank you for this?"

"Give me a chance. That's all I want, sweetheart. Just a chance to show you what our life together could be like. This is just a sample."

"Not every day can be like this."

"Maybe not, but we could give it a hell of a shot.

There are so many things I'd like to do for you, so many places I'd like to share.''

Warning bells rang dimly in the back of her mind, but for once Garrett pretended not to hear them. "Tell me about them, Joshua. Tell me about your life.''

As they glided across the snow and day turned into dusk, he told her about a world filled with exotic, fascinating places she'd only read about, adventures she'd only dreamed of. It was an alluring world. The images he painted teased her mind, the way his touches teased her flesh.

"Have there been a lot of women in your life?''

"Millions.''

"I'm serious.''

"None to compare to you.'' He tilted her face up until her mouth was only a hairbreadth away. "None,'' he said again and fit his lips to hers. The velvet caress was convincing. The ragged pace of his pulse, when she touched her fingers to his neck, was even more so. A woman could believe in a man whose kisses heated like fire and tasted of chocolate. *She* could believe in *this man.*

But, dear Lord, how afraid she was. She looked into Joshua's eyes and saw love. She looked again and saw commitment. Then she looked into her own heart and the fear didn't seem nearly as real as his kisses and the promise in his eyes.

"A chance,'' he whispered. "Is that so terribly difficult for you?''

It was terrifying...or had been mere hours ago. Now it seemed possible. "I'll try," she vowed.

Joshua's arms stole around her in an undemanding hug that was far more compelling than the hottest passion. There was understanding in that hug and yet another promise. Garrett had rarely trusted promises. She had long since sworn off risks. Tonight it seemed her world was undergoing a change that was likely to affect the rest of her life.

The sight that greeted Joshua when he entered the kitchen brought laughter bubbling up from deep inside him. Wisely, he choked it off as he watched Garrett struggling to stir a lump of flour and milk into what he supposed was biscuit dough. She was scowling fiercely at the mess.

"Having an attack of domesticity, are we?" he inquired, probably a shade too cheerfully. She glowered at him.

"Elena's sick," she reported succinctly.

"So you're cooking dinner?"

"Don't sound so horrified."

"Horrified, no. Curious, yes. What exactly is that you're beating to death?"

"Biscuits," she said, confirming his original guess.

"Don't beat them," he suggested, keeping his voice bland. "They'll be tough."

"I suppose you could do better."

"I could."

She poked the bowl at him, which was no mean feat

considering the size of the ceramic dish. "Be my guest."

"Ask nicely."

"I just did."

He grinned. "I don't think so. It sounded more like a challenge to me."

"And you don't rise to challenges?"

"Oh, I rise to most anything that intrigues me. In this instance, though, I think I'd prefer a small bribe."

She regarded him suspiciously. "Such as?"

"A kiss."

"Oh, no. Kisses with you have a way of leading into dangerous territory." A delightful blush crept into her cheeks.

He grinned. "Yes, they do, don't they? Be realistic, though. If I have to get dinner on the table for a dozen people, I won't have much time to follow through on that one little kiss."

Her eyes lit up and she asked thoughtfully, "You'll do the whole dinner?"

"Every course. Rare prime rib. Caesar salad. Mashed potatoes and gravy. Green beans almandine. Biscuits. Maybe even a cherry cobbler with cream." He drew the list out slowly, tantalizing her with the images. She was practically licking her very desirable lips when he added, "If I like the way you kiss."

She blinked and shook her head. "You'll do all that for one kiss?"

"Just think what I'd do if you threw in a hug."

She set the bowl on the counter with a decisive thud

and crossed the room in three quick, decisive steps, her cast thumping on the tile floor. Before he realized what she meant to do, she'd pecked him lightly on the cheek, grabbed her jacket and headed for the door. "Thanks," she called over her shoulder, her expression very sassy and self-satisfied.

"Whoa!" He snagged a corner of her jacket and brought her to a halt.

Eyes wide, she stared back at him. "Yes?"

"That kiss won't even get the roast in the oven." He used her jacket like a rope to tug her closer. "Now, this is the sort of kiss I had in mind."

His lips slowly settled on hers, teasing, coaxing, re-kindling the quick velvet heat of desire. He lingered to learn the shape of her mouth, to rediscover the sweet, sweet taste of her. After one startled gasp, she fell victim to his touch, melting in his arms, sliding her arms around his neck, threading her fingers through his hair. The temperature in the kitchen rose a good twenty degrees. A few more and that lump of dough wouldn't need the oven to bake.

When he finally released her, she very nearly sagged into the nearest chair. "For that kiss you ought to cook for the next month."

"If you think I'm going to feed a dozen ranch hands, including the man who's half in love with you, for a month, you're crazy. You'd have to go for a lot more than one paltry, old kiss."

"That kiss was not paltry," she retorted, looking offended.

"I suppose you can do better?"

"Of course I can," she said before her eyes blinked wide. "I mean..."

"Oh no, sweetheart. You said it. Let's see you back it up." He stood nobly in front of her. "I'm ready."

She sniffed. "You look as if you're about to make some supreme sacrifice."

"I'll tell you after the kiss how much of a sacrifice it was."

"Joshua Ames, if you think you can goad me into kissing you again, you are out of your mind."

"Coward."

"Am not."

"Then let's see you pucker up, darlin'."

"I suppose you won't be satisfied until you get me into your bed again."

"Now that's an intriguing thought."

"One which I'm sure you never considered." There was the tiniest hint of sarcasm in her voice, but amusement danced in her eyes.

"Never," he said piously. "I am an honorable man. I will wed you."

He saw the quick flicker of fear, but she kept her voice emphatic. "Over my dead body."

"You would give up the chance to experience my culinary skills for the rest of your life?"

"I haven't even experienced them for dinner. Maybe you'd better get through this trial run. Then we'll see if we have anything to talk about."

"I have other talents deserving of a trial run," he offered generously.

Her gaze narrowed. "I've sampled those."

"And?"

"The jury's still out," she said sassily, ducking past him and heading for the door.

This time he let her go. If he hadn't, dinner would have been hours late and he'd have had a dozen ravenous ranch hands to fend off. Besides, it was more than enough that he'd planted the seductive notion in Garrett's mind. He knew it would nag at her for days now. Anticipation was sometimes every bit as sweet as the lovemaking.

Chapter Twelve

Joshua and Mrs. Mac were up to something. Garrett watched their conspiratorial looks, their whispered conversations and grew increasingly suspicious. They had finally stopped hovering over her once the doctor had assured them that her ankle was healing nicely and would be in its cast no more than another week or so. They hadn't even objected too strenuously when she'd decided to move back to her own house. In fact, Joshua had barely seemed to react to the announcement at all. His suddenly disinterested attitude irked her almost as much as knowing he was just down the hall had previously provoked her.

"I'm going," she announced from the foyer, her small bag sitting by her feet. They barely even looked up. Joshua did manage a distracted wave.

"I'll be back next year," she said and waited for the flurry of commotion to begin.

"Okay," Mrs. Mac said mildly. Joshua never even glanced at her.

Thoroughly miffed now, Garrett stepped into the room, walked over until she was practically under their noses, in fact. "Okay, that's it," she announced. "What the hell is going on around here?"

Two pairs of innocent eyes stared up at her.

Mrs. Mac's face creased in a worried frown. "Garrett, dear, is something the matter?"

Hands on hips, she glared at the two of them. "You tell me."

They exchanged a look. "We're just making a few plans," Mrs. Mac said.

"Nothing that you need to worry about," Joshua added.

"What if I want to worry?" she countered, only one step away from a childish pout.

A grin tugged at Joshua's lips. "Feeling left out, are you?"

"I just think I have a right to know if something's going on. I am supposed to be the manager of this ranch."

"Oh, this isn't ranch business, dear." Mrs. Mac patted her hand.

Defeated, Garrett began backing toward the door. "Never mind, then."

Joshua grabbed her wrist and tried pulling her into

his lap. She resisted. He tugged harder and finally tumbled her into his arms.

"Oh, for heaven's sakes," he said, amusement radiating from every rotten pore of him. "Let's just tell her."

Mrs. Mac looked thoughtful. "I suppose she will have to be told sooner or later, but I was hoping we could surprise her."

Garrett's eyes blinked wide and she pushed herself up from the awkward position in which she'd landed. It was not *really* intentional that she put her hand smack in Joshua's face for leverage. She addressed her questions directly to Mrs. Mac, who in the long run was a far more trustworthy source than the unscrupulous man holding her. "A surprise? For me? Why?"

"Well, your birthday is coming, dear. What do you think, Joshua? Should we tell her and spoil the surprise?"

Still rubbing his nose, which she'd mashed, he studied her intently. Finally he shook his head. "I don't think so."

Garrett tumbled out of his lap, grabbed a pillow from the sofa and threw it at him. Laughing, he caught in in mid-air. "Okay. Okay. You tell her, though. I need to focus all my attention on fending off another one of her sneak attacks. The woman can't stay away from me."

"You wish. Now talk."

"We're planning a party," Mrs. Mac announced.

Garrett blinked. "A party?"

Joshua rolled his eyes. "You know, one of those events where people get together, eat a lot of food, dance a little, tell jokes, put lampshades on their heads."

Mrs. Mac grimaced at Joshua's description. "My lampshades will remain precisely where they are," she warned.

"Don't tell me," he said. "I would never dream of doing anything so juvenile." His gaze shifted to Garrett. "But some of your guests might."

"Sometimes, you are thoroughly obnoxious," Garrett pointed out. It didn't seem to faze him. "Why are you having the party?"

"I told you, dear. It's for your birthday. It was Joshua's idea."

She regarded him suspiciously. "Why?"

His expression suddenly turned serious. The intensity of his gaze pinned her like a doe caught in headlights. His voice dropped to a husky whisper. "So I can get you into my arms on a dance floor and make love to you to the music all night long."

The provocative image ripped through her and left her knees trembling.

"Joshua," she objected weakly. She shot a look at Mrs. Mac to see how she was taking this blatantly sexual announcement. Instead of outright shock, she saw an unfamiliar dreaminess in those bright blue eyes.

"Oh, my," Mrs. Mac said finally. "Young man, you certainly know how to bring back memories."

She watched as Joshua reached over and gently

squeezed a gnarled hand. "I expect you to save a dance for me, too," he told the older woman.

A spark of pure devilment crept into those old eyes. "Just watch where you put those wicked hands of yours, young man."

Garrett was able to pry very little additional information out of the two of them. Not even Elena, who was back to bustling about in the kitchen again, would reveal much. That night at dinner in her own house again, Garrett decided to see how much her daughter knew about the upcoming event.

"Casey, what have you heard about this party that Mrs. Mac is planning?"

Casey looked startled. "You know?"

"I know they're planning it. They wouldn't tell me any of the details."

"Did you tell them you wouldn't come?"

"No. Why would I do that?"

"I thought you didn't want to spend time with Joshua."

Garrett listened as her own advice came back to haunt her. "Sweetie, there's a big difference between going to a party and being involved with someone."

"What about the sleigh ride?"

"How on earth did you know about that?"

"Elena told me. I saddled up Bright Lightning and went for a ride to see if it was true." Accusing eyes glared at her. "Mom, you were kissing him."

She couldn't very well deny what Casey had seen with her own eyes, though she very much wanted to.

"I know. I can't explain it, but it seemed like the right thing to do at the time."

A faint spark of hope flickered in Casey's eyes. "Does that mean you're going to date him, after all?"

Dating seemed an innocuous term for what had been happening lately between her and Joshua. Too cautious to label it more, she simply nodded. "While he's here," she was quick to point out. "I don't expect it to last once he's gone home again."

Although Garrett had made the claim aloud, she believed it the way an eight-year-old denied a belief in Santa Claus, with more hope of being wrong than certainty of being right. She did want it to last. She was beginning to dream of happily ever afters. She just wasn't going to admit it. If nothing else, she would salvage her pride when he'd gone.

Disappointment written on her face, Casey pushed her plate away. "May I be excused?"

"When you've finished your dinner."

"I'm not hungry. If I have to sit here a week, I still won't be hungry."

Since Casey was perfectly capable of making good on her claim through sheer stubbornness, Garrett sighed and waved her off. "See that your homework's done before you watch any TV."

Just then the back door opened simultaneously with a knock. Heart galloping, Garrett met Joshua's gaze. "Afraid to risk waiting for me to let you in?"

"Just saving your bad ankle. Hi, Casey, how are

you? You haven't been around much the last few days.''

Casey shrugged and stared at her uneaten meat loaf. ''I've had homework.''

''Want to take a break tonight and play a little chess with me?''

She shook her head and edged toward the door. ''Too much homework,'' she mumbled and took off.

Joshua watched her go with troubled eyes. ''Have you talked to her about this?'' he asked Garrett.

''It'll pass.''

He shook his head. ''I don't think so. I think it's gone on long enough.''

''Where are you going?''

''To talk to her.''

''Joshua!'' The protest was wasted. He was already through the door. She could hear his footsteps taking the stairs two at a time and winced. If Casey actually answered his questions, they would probably hear his roar of fury halfway to Montana. In fact, she wondered if there was any way to get safely across the state line in the next half hour.

Lines from *King Lear* about the sharp tongues of thankless children came to mind. She had a feeling she was about to discover exactly what Shakespeare had had in mind when he'd written them.

Joshua tapped lightly on Casey's bedroom door and waited. Finally he heard a very reluctant ''Come in.''

He cracked the door and saw that she was sitting at her desk, a wary expression on her face.

"Could we talk, kiddo?"

"About what?"

"Why you seem to be so mad at me?"

A sigh shuddered through her and her shoulders sagged. The look she directed at him was filled with guilt. "I'm not mad exactly."

"Then let's talk about what you are exactly." He sat down on the edge of her bed, faintly intimidated by the ruffled canopy and collection of dolls. He wasn't used to all these feminine frills. "Want to sit over here by me?"

Casey approached him cautiously and picked a spot near the head of the bed. She picked up one of the dolls, a well-worn baby doll with faded clothes and skimpy hair. Clutching it to her chest, she waited patiently. Joshua could see a whole ton of emotions in her demeanor—anxiety, caution, and an oddly grown-up calm. If she hadn't been clinging so desperately to that ragged doll or if he hadn't seen the storm raging in her eyes, he might have bought her serene facade. Suddenly faced with this girl, who was part child, part woman, Joshua grew nervous. He wasn't at all sure where to start.

"What's been happening with you lately?" he began innocuously enough.

She seemed relieved not to be asked a direct question about the cause of her anger. "You know, school, chores, stuff like that."

"You haven't been around the house much. I gather you've been eating your meals with the hands."

"Mom said it would be okay," she said defensively.

"Of course, it is. I just wondered why you didn't want to eat up at the house with us."

She shrugged and gazed at the floor.

"Okay, let's back up a minute. This goes back to that morning in the hospital, doesn't it?"

Her gaze shot to his, then skittered away. "I don't know what you mean."

"I think you do. You and your mother argued about something that day, didn't you? Was it about me?"

Joshua could hear the ticking of the huge, old-fashioned alarm clock sitting on the nightstand. It seemed an eternity passed before she nodded.

Biting back anger, he asked calmly, "Want to tell me about it?"

"Mom says you're going back to Florida," she mumbled.

With that single revelation, Joshua understood it all. Garrett had planted her own seeds of doubt in her daughter's fertile imagination. "You're afraid I'll leave you."

"And Mom."

"Casey, at some point, I will go back. I can't deny that. I have a business there."

A tear trickled down her cheek. With fingers that suddenly seemed all thumbs, he reached over and brushed it away. "No tears, okay. Casey, look at me."

Eyes shimmering with tears, she glanced up finally.

"Honey, I will always, *always,* come back."

"But you told me you wanted to marry Mom. You can't marry her and be gone all the time, can you? What kind of family would that be?"

He sighed and took her hand between his. "I don't have all the answers yet. I'm still not even certain if your mother wants me around on a permanent basis. Once she and I have worked that part out, I promise you, if it is within my power, we will be a family, all in the same place."

"Promise?"

"I promise."

"Are you going to ask her to marry you at the party?"

He grinned. "That is between your mother and me."

"Oh," she said, clearly disappointed.

"But I could use a little help in picking out her present. Want to go into Cheyenne with me on Saturday to find something?"

Her eyes lit up. "Really? You mean it? Just the two of us?"

"Just the two of us. We'll make a day of it. Shopping, lunch, the works."

"A movie?"

He grinned at her enthusiasm. "Why not?"

He reached across then and hugged her. "That's my girl. The next time you're worried about what's going on with me, you just ask, okay?"

"I'm sorry I doubted you."

"I'm just glad we worked it out. I've missed our

chess games. You're the only competition around. Mrs. Mac really is lousy,'' he confided. ''Just don't tell her I said so.''

Giggling, she hugged him back. ''I won't. I promise.''

On his way downstairs it took everything in Joshua to keep his temper under control. The way Garrett had managed to twist things for Casey infuriated him. It was bad enough that she hadn't allowed any of his efforts to make a dent in her distrust, but to destroy Casey's faith in him was unconscionable.

He found her pacing the kitchen, limping back and forth on her walking cast and casting nervous glances toward the doorway. ''You should be scared,'' he said mildly.

''What did she tell you?''

''The truth. She said you'd told her I was leaving, that she shouldn't count on me for anything.''

Garrett's jaw set stubbornly. ''I told her that for her own good. She can't count on anyone except herself.''

''And me,'' he said furiously. ''And Mrs. Mac and you. Or don't you believe you all qualify, either?''

''Of course, it's just that…''

''Just what? That I'm a man? That I don't live here? That I'm not her real father? Is that what this is really all about, Garrett? Are you still in love with the man who got you pregnant and then deserted you?''

''No-o-o.'' Her eyes wide with shock, she stammered over the too quick denial. ''Of course not.''

He shook his head. ''I'm not so sure. There's a

mighty fine line between love and hate. Maybe you ought to take a good, hard look and see which side your feelings for that man fall on. While you're at it, take a look at what you're feeling for me. I'm not a patient man, Garrett. You've stretched me just about to my limit. You sit on the fence much longer and I just might not be around when you decide to jump down.''

On his way to the door he stopped just long enough to place a hard, bruising kiss on her suddenly vulnerable mouth. He wanted her to remember what was real, what was lasting.

He wanted her to remember him.

[text faded and illegible]

Chapter Thirteen

Garrett had never seen the house in such a state of chaos. Mrs. Mac had hired extra help to shine the floors, polish the chandeliers and help Elena in the kitchen in preparation for what seemed to be turning into an extraordinarily lavish birthday party.

All of the feverish activity only underscored Garrett's own restlessness. She couldn't concentrate. Memories of Joshua's warning taunted her day and night. He had been amazingly tolerant of her uncertainties. He'd even seemed to forgive her, if only barely, for upsetting Casey with dire predictions about his departure. The man was a saint, she thought crankily. All that generosity of spirit was tough to ignore, though she was certainly trying. The fact that her blood sizzled when he came into a room only compounded the problem she seemed to be having with her common sense.

Just then her pulse skipped a beat and she knew intuitively that Joshua had entered the room. Her whole body came alive in his presence, tingling, anticipating.

"Ready?" he asked, and again her heartbeat accelerated, though she knew rationally that the question was perfectly innocuous. The man was only taking her to the doctor to get her cast removed.

She should have been thrilled. She would finally be able to get around easily on her own again. Instead she had these crazy mixed feelings. Over the last weeks she'd grown accustomed to Joshua's gentleness. Though she'd fought him tooth and nail, deep down she'd enjoyed being taken care of. The breakfast and lunch trays in bed, the sleigh ride, the long quiet talks, all had finally bewitched her. She'd been able to justify her response by reminding herself repeatedly that it was just temporary, only until the cast came off. Now, perversely, she discovered she didn't want that incredible, cherished feeling to end. That was a dangerous, dismaying discovery for a woman who prided herself on needing no one.

"I'm ready," she said, turning around finally, praying that he couldn't read her confusion in her eyes.

"What is it?" he asked at once.

"What is what?"

"There's something wrong. You're crying."

Her fingers flew to her cheek. To her astonishment, she realized he was right. She really was coming unglued. Wiping the dampness away, she said, "Sorry, I didn't even realize."

At the tiny catch in her voice, he was across the room in three strides, pulling her into his arms. Nestled against his chest, that cherished sensation flooded through her again. Joshua represented strength and caring, two of the things most lacking throughout her entire life. Listening to the steady rhythm of his heart, feeling the power of its beat, a surprising reassurance swept over her. This wasn't Casey's father. This wasn't an immature boy who would walk out on her, leaving her heart in tatters. This was a man she could love through all eternity...if only she dared.

A sigh whispered through her and Joshua's arms tightened. "Garrett?"

"I'm okay," she said finally, stepping back. She saw the damage her tears had done to his shirt. "You, on the other hand, are a mess. Let me have that shirt and I'll get Elena to dry it and iron it for you."

A flicker of pure mischief dashed through his eyes as he reached for the buttons. "I think I like this crying stuff, after all."

Her gaze narrowed suspiciously. "Because?"

"You've never asked me to take off my clothes before."

"Joshua, I am not asking you to take off your clothes," she retorted even as she watched him dutifully unbutton his shirt. Her protest was entirely too weak. "I just meant..."

"Oh, I know what you meant. Normally you're just

too shy to ask. Now you have an excuse." He stripped the shirt away and threw it over the chair, then reached for the waistband of his jeans.

"Don't you dare!" she ordered, but it was more whisper than command. Her eyes were locked on the breadth of his bare chest.

"But…" Joshua implored with all innocence.

Swallowing hard, she dragged her gaze up to challenge his. "If you even think about touching that zipper, I'm out of here."

Disappointment streaked across his face. "Too bad," he said, snapping the jeans closed just as Mrs. Mac came into the room and gasped.

"Oh, my," she said breathlessly. The starch was back in her voice in no more than a heartbeat. "Joshua Ames, put your clothes on right this instant. Garrett, I'm surprised at you. Casey could have been the one walking in here instead of me."

"It's…it's not the way it looks," Garrett explained hurriedly. "Joshua's shirt got wet. He was just taking it off so Elena could dry it."

"Humph!" Her expression was disbelieving.

"True," Joshua said. "Much to my dismay, our intentions were purely innocent."

"I doubt you were innocent the day you hit the cradle, young man. Wet or not, I suggest you put that shirt back on until you get another one from upstairs."

With a wink at Garrett, he put it back on every bit as slowly as he'd taken it off. To her dismay, she watched every bit as avidly as she had his disrobing.

"Come on, sweetheart. Let's get to that doctor. I can't wait to watch you taking something off."

"Joshua!" She shot a worried look at Mrs. Mac, but she was chuckling.

"The cast, darlin'. The cast."

"Oh," she said and could have kicked herself for not keeping the disappointment out of her voice. The man was entirely too smug without her giving him more to gloat over.

"I like you in pink," he noted. "What do you think, Mrs. Mac?"

"Very becoming."

Garrett glanced down at her red shirt and blue jeans. "Pink?"

"Your cheeks." His grin widened. "Fascinating. Now they match that shirt."

She glared at him. "I wonder if Red would drive me to the doctor."

Before she realized what he intended, she was off the floor and in Joshua's arms. He glowered fiercely. "Not likely. You and I have a date and I get real testy when a lady stands me up."

"Has anyone ever dared?"

He considered the question thoughtfully. "Not since the first grade Halloween party. Lynda Dixon."

"You still remember her name?"

"A man's not likely to forget a woman who rejects him."

"Obviously she was a very shortsighted woman."

"Exactly what I told her when she begged me to take her to the senior prom."

Laughing, she settled comfortably in his arms. "Okay. Okay. I get the picture."

He nodded approvingly. "I thought you might."

Joshua's grip on the phone tightened. This was the last thing he needed. After weeks of delicate maneuvers to assure Garrett of his feelings, he couldn't leave Wyoming now. She'd never trust him again. Now that she was out of that cast and on her own two feet, she'd take off on him like a shot at the first hint of what she perceived of betrayal. "Suzy, tell him I'll be back in a week or two," he told his assistant. "Reschedule the appointment."

"He's adamant, boss. You'll see him by the first of the week or he'll hire someone else."

Joshua wanted to tell the man to go to blazes, but he didn't dare. Not that he couldn't sacrifice this account and a dozen more. He didn't need their money. However, he did need to keep his reputation for reliability intact. That, every bit as much as his financial skill, was what kept him in business as an investment consultant. Obviously he'd put off this prospective client just as long as he could.

"Tell him I'll meet with him on Monday morning. I'll fly back late Sunday."

"I'll take care of it," Suzy said.

"Anything else?"

"Nothing I can't handle. Is everything okay out there? Are Mrs. McDonald's finances untangled yet?"

"As much as they're ever likely to be. I think she'd be content to keep her spare cash in a cookie jar, if she weren't so set on amassing a fortune to leave to Cal."

"A fortune he doesn't want or need. The only thing that man needs is family. Can't she see that?"

"Maybe if he'd stay out here for more than fifteen minutes at a time, she'd realize it. Instead, the harder she tries to bribe him into staying, the quicker he is to run."

"Maybe this time'll be different. Cal called this morning and said he and Marilou were leaving for the ranch at noon. He wanted to know if there was anything you wanted me to send along with him. I told him I'd just sent you half a dozen faxes and that anything else could wait until you got back."

"You didn't know I'd be coming back Monday."

"Sure I did," she said. "I can read you like a book. I'd already made your plane reservations, but Cal said you could fly back with them."

Joshua chuckled ruefully. "It's nice to know I'm so predictable."

"Not that predictable," she assured him. "For instance, I would have sworn you'd be back two minutes after you landed. Guess you hadn't gotten that cowgirl out of your system, after all."

"What do you know about Garrett?"

This time Suzy laughed. "Come on, boss. I can add two and two as well as you can. See you Monday."

"Yeah," he grumbled. "See you Monday. Maybe I'll surprise you and be late."

"That wouldn't just surprise me. It would send me into shock. Bye-bye."

Joshua would have growled something about the fate of disrespectful help, but she'd already hung up in his ear. Instead he simply sat and stared out the window. His fingers curled around the jewelry box in his pocket. He'd bought the engagement ring on his shopping trip with Casey. She'd helped him pick it out. The blue star sapphire shimmered like lights. The diamonds around it glistened like stars in a midnight sky. The ring had reminded him of the dazzle in Garrett's eyes when she had stared up at him in the heat of passion. He'd known at once that a simple diamond would never do. He planned to give it to her tomorrow night. With any luck the birthday party would turn into an engagement celebration. Now he wondered how much celebration he could hope for, once she learned that he was about to go back to Florida.

Garrett stood in front of the full-length mirror and slowly turned. She couldn't believe that the woman reflected in the glass was really her. The blue satin dress bared shoulders that were pale as cream. The hem skimmed her knees, displaying slender calves and well-turned ankles. She could barely tell that she'd just had a cast removed from one leg, though she had been forced to wear flat shoes rather than the heels that would have been more traditional with the gown. Over her objections, Casey had brushed her hair until it hung in a shiny wave below her shoulders. It was caught back from her face on one side by a rhinestone studded comb lent by Mrs. McDonald. The two of them had pronounced her *gorgeous* thirty minutes ago. She still couldn't quite get over the possibility that they might be right.

There was a tap on the door. Expecting Joshua, she called out, her gaze still fastened on her reflection. A soft, wolf whistle shimmered across her nerves. A thousand butterflies took flight in her stomach. She turned slow and found not Joshua, but Marilou Rivers, Cal's wife.

"Stay away from my husband," Marilou said, but her eyes were sparkling with amusement and there was an approving smile on her lips. "You look drop-dead gorgeous. Joshua won't know what hit him."

"Are you sure?" Garrett said, her voice filled with uncertainty. "It's not too much?"

"Maybe for a rodeo, but this is a party. You look perfect."

"Like a lady?" she said wryly. "That's what my daughter said. She sounded stunned."

"You know, Garrett, being a survivor and being a lady aren't incompatible. It's just a matter of balance."

"Maybe. Sometimes, though, I think what Joshua really needs is someone who's all woman."

Marilou chuckled. "I suspect you're as much woman as he could ever hope to handle. Just because you put on jeans and live on a ranch doesn't mean you can't be feminine underneath. Since Cal and I got married and I found myself living on a Thoroughbred farm, I've taken to wearing the frilliest lace underwear I can find. The first time he discovered that he almost had a coronary. Now every time he sees me in those pants, all he remembers is what I'm wearing under them. Believe me, he never forgets for one single second that I'm a woman.''

Garrett wondered if Joshua always remembered her lace underwear and pink toenail polish when he discovered her in the barn with hay in her hair and dirt streaking her face. Maybe tonight she'd be able to give him new memories to cling to during those times when she was dusty and tired from a roundup. Maybe it was possible to give Joshua the lady he needed without losing her sense of self in the process.

Impulsively she hugged Marilou. ''Thank you.''

''For what?''

''For making a future for Joshua and me seem almost possible.''

There was another tap on the door and this time it was Cal who stuck his head in and whistled. ''Wow! Two of the prettiest women in town and they're hiding out upstairs. Joshua come see the transformation.''

Marilou gave him a mock glare. ''I thought you said I was always beautiful.''

''Oh, you are,'' he said hurriedly, winking at Garrett. ''Must be that the color you're wearing is particularly flattering.''

''Quick thinking,'' Joshua said approvingly as his

gaze sought Garrett, who was still standing in the background. When he found her, his eyes widened. Cal and Marilou chuckled.

"Well, he's down for the count," Cal said. "Come on, wife. I think I hear our names being called from downstairs. We'd better get there before Grandmother hires an architect to build that house for us."

When they had gone, Joshua stepped into the room and held out his hands. "Come, let me look at you."

Garrett took his hands and held on tight.

"Scared?"

"A little."

"Sweetheart, these are your friends downstairs."

"But I'm used to running into them in a diner or maybe at the feed store. I'm out of my element on a dance floor."

"You wouldn't be out of your element at the White House. I'm very proud to have you on my arm. Now let's get going before Cal eats all the food."

"Cal and an entire army couldn't eat all the food Elena and the caterer have prepared."

"Elena? I thought the caterer was doing it all?"

"She wasn't convinced he'd make quite enough. Truthfully, I think she was feeling left out. Mrs. Mac wanted her to feel like a guest tonight, but she was still refusing to leave the kitchen last time I checked."

"How close did you come to refusing to leave the barn?"

"It crossed my mind, but I figured you and Mrs. Mac would have a posse out after me."

His gaze lingered on the bare curve of her shoulder, then drifted to the swell of her breast. "There is something to be said about the barn," he murmured, his breathing a little faster.

"Not on your life. I didn't get all dolled up to go tumbling into a haystack. Let's go, Mr. Ames." She tucked her arm through his and went with him downstairs. Halfway down she realized that the dozen or so early arrivals were all standing at the bottom, all eyes on their descent. It was a wonder she didn't trip and land in their midst. Joshua gave her fingers a reassuring squeeze.

"Showtime, darlin'. You're going to knock 'em dead."

The only impression Garrett really worried about, though, was the one she made on the man by her side. The fact that she cared so much worried her. Her gaze rose to meet Joshua's and found the sought-after approval blazing in his eyes. Her confidence soared.

"You're the most handsome man in the room," she confided, lacing her fingers through his. "I'm very glad to be your date."

With his gaze locked on hers, he whispered, "We're going to make it a night to remember."

After that, everything became a blur. It was nearly midnight when the pace slowed and the band finally struck up the promised waltz. Garrett had sensed Joshua's increasing frustration with the lively square dances that had filled the evening. Every time the caller had insisted that he change partners, he'd done so with obvious reluctance. His possessive gaze had never strayed from her, especially when she'd been hand-in-hand with Red. Even now he still didn't fully realize that he had nothing to fear from the foreman. She thought of Red as a wonderful friend, an older brother almost, but nothing more.

Now, though, the first note of the waltz floated on the air and with a gleam in his eyes, Joshua held out his arms. "This is our dance, darlin'."

Garrett stepped into the embrace, her heart thundering in her chest as his hands settled on her hips and fit them snugly against him.

"Watch it," she whispered in his ear. "Mrs. Mac will be over here with a ruler in a minute to see that you keep a proper distance between us."

"She wouldn't dare. I've been waiting all night to hold you like this." He leaned back just enough to look into her eyes. "Happy?"

"Incredibly," she said and rested her head on his chest. "It's been an evening of magic."

"That's just what I promised. It could be like this always."

Oh, how she wanted to believe that. If anyone could convince her, Joshua could. "Always is a very long time."

"But I'm very good at making magic."

"You have an ego the size of Texas."

"It's not ego if it's fact."

"Then it's just plain old bragging," she teased, her fingers weaving through the hair that had grown long enough to brush the collar of his shirt. Heat flared in his eyes.

"You still enjoy taunting me, don't you?"

"As hobbies go, I'll admit I could find at least a dozen that would be far more boring."

"There's a real streak of vamp in you, did you realize that?"

"Is that good?"

He pulled her close again, until his very heat seemed to radiate around her. "Can't you tell how good that is?"

With a sense of shock, she realized exactly how aroused he was.

"I need you, Garrett. Come away with me."

"Now?" Longing and the sweet tension throbbing through her warred with duty. She couldn't disappear from her own party.

"Tomorrow."

Puzzled she stared at him. There was an unreadable look in his eyes. "Why tomorrow?"

For a moment there was only the rhythmic rise and fall of the music, the gentle sway of their bodies. She could feel his tension, though, and suddenly the worst fear she had ever known spread through her.

She pulled back and accused, "You're leaving, aren't you? You're going back to Florida tomorrow?"

Joshua's arms merely tightened around her.

"Joshua?"

He sighed deeply. "Yes. There's a meeting on Monday. I have to be there. I have a responsibility to my other clients. I've neglected them for far too long.''

"Then by all means go," she said tightly. "I wouldn't want to stop you."

She jerked free and ran through the house; Joshua was right on her heels. If it hadn't been for that damned ankle, she would have beat him. Instead he caught up with her just outside.

"Garrett, you have to listen to me."

Her whole body tensed when he touched her. Slowly he turned her around until she was facing him. Her chin rose a notch and she prayed he wouldn't see the way it quivered. "Why should I listen?" she demanded. "We all knew this moment was going to come. Go. You don't owe me a thing."

"No," he said softly. "I don't owe you anything, but I do love you."

"But you love your job more."

"More?" he said. "You think I love it more than you? More than this?"

He crushed her lips beneath his. Garrett's breath seemed to die in her throat as he plundered her mouth. She wanted to fight him. She even made one half-hearted attempt to push him away, but the blazing desire that fueled the kiss was persuasive. With a sigh, she gave in to the heat that swirled through her. She twined her arms around his neck and took all that he had to offer. A raging hunger made her needy. Fear made her desperate. He was going to go and there would be no more nights like this, no more kisses, no more gentle caresses or seductive touches. She would be alone again. In that instant of realization, she hated him. She hated him for giving her all of this and then taking it away.

She lifted her hands and touched his face, memorizing the faint lines, the purely male texture, that intriguing hint of some long-ago fight that marred the perfection. A great sadness settled over her.

"Garrett, marry me. Come with me to Florida."

For one heart-stopping minute the only thing that registered was the proposal. *Marry me. Marry me.* Joy began to build, chasing away the fear, chasing away the sorrow. Then the rest of his words sank in. He wanted her to leave this place, this haven. He was asking her to give up everything she had fought so hard for. How could he do that, if he truly loved her?

"No," she said. "I can't go to Florida with you. I love you, Joshua, but my life is here."

"Just think about it."

"There's no point," she told him flatly. "Everything I need is here."

"Not everything. Whether you're ready to admit it or not, you need me, too. One of these days, you'll have to admit that. I just hope it's before it's too late."

She shook her head. "I love you, Joshua, but I will never, *ever* need you. I won't ever need anyone again."

He smiled at her wearily. "Maybe one of these days, you'll see that the two go hand in hand." He pressed a chaste kiss on her forehead. "I'll say goodbye before I leave."

She nodded, then forced herself to stand perfectly still and watch him walk away. Only when he had gone did she allow the first sob to escape. She turned and fled to her house in search of the serenity it had always given her in the past. Tonight, though, the rooms seemed filled with ghostly reminders that she was losing something she might never find again.

Chapter Fourteen

The wind set up an eerie howling. It seemed like an eternity had passed since he'd watched Garrett go into her house. Joshua remained in the shadows, ignoring the freezing night air as he started after her. In his pocket, his fingers curled around the sapphire engagement ring. He should have given it to her. Maybe then she would have believed in him. Wasn't that what a ring was all about, a symbol of love, of commitment? Maybe it would have made a difference.

Then he recalled the bleak expression in her eyes, the shadow of pain, the accusing hint of betrayal. He sighed deeply and admitted that bits of glass and metal, no matter how precious, would be meaningless to a woman who wouldn't allow herself to trust anyone. If all these weeks had meant so little to her, there was nothing he could say now to convince her how much he loved her.

A faint whisper of cigarette smoke told him that Cal had joined him. Obviously, Marilou hadn't caught him or that cigarette would have been history.

"What's up, pal? Did Cinderella leave the ball?" Cal asked.

"Something like that."

Side by side, lost in their own thoughts, they stood silently for a time until Cal finally said, "You're in love with her, aren't you? Marilou thinks you have been for a long time."

Joshua sighed. "Since the first time I laid eyes on her, I suppose. I was planning to ask her to marry me tonight."

"But you didn't."

"The timing seemed all wrong. I have to fly home tomorrow and she thinks I'm leaving for good. I tried to get her to come along, but that only made matters worse."

"Could be that she thinks you expect her to give up her life here. Do you?"

"Would that be so wrong?" he asked angrily. "We could have a wonderful life in Florida. She'd never have to work another day in her life."

"With any other woman that might be the perfect gift. It might even be the case with Garrett, once you've given her some time to adjust to the idea of being idle. I don't know her well, but from what

Grandmother has told me, she's a woman who very much needs to feel she's in control of her own destiny. There's nothing scarier to someone like that than trusting her fate to another person."

Joshua studied his friend's face. "Speaking from experience?"

"Absolutely. From the day we met, Marilou always knew what was best for me, how much I needed to feel a part of a family again. I was just too bullheaded to admit it. Once I did, life got a whole lot easier."

"How'd she persuade you?"

"Patience. Persistence." He grinned. "And the sweetest damned kisses I'd ever known." He squeezed Joshua's shoulder. "In fact, I think that little temptress is waiting for me now. If you have to leave tomorrow, fly back with us, okay? Play your cards right and I'll even let you hold the baby."

Joshua grinned at the totally bewitched tone in Cal's voice. "Is that supposed to entice me?" he teased. "Or scare me to death?"

"Trust me on this. You'll never experience anything like holding one of your own. I didn't think it was possible to feel an emotion that powerful. Maybe a sample will give you the patience and persistence you'll need to stick with Garrett for the long haul. You coming in now?"

"Not quite yet. Thanks for the talk, though."

"Anytime, pal. Anytime."

Eventually, when the chill reached deep into his very soul, Joshua went inside, but he didn't sleep. He spent the next hour prowling the house, hovering near the window that allowed him a view of Garrett's place and wondering if they were truly meant to be, after all.

When the waiting and worrying finally got to be too much for him, he began to pack. It didn't take nearly long enough. He carried his bags down to the foyer and placed them by the door. He would have left right then, but his promise to Garrett held him back. He had told her he would come by to say goodbye. If he failed even at that, she would convince herself that all the rest had been lies, as well.

At loose ends until the rest of the household awoke hours from now, he suddenly remembered the cabin. He and Garrett had shared only one night there, but they had been happy. It was the night he had discovered he was capable of love. It was the night Garrett had lost herself to passion, had dared to let him see her vulnerability. He needed to recapture that fleeting moment of trust, needed to remind himself of what he'd been fighting for. Recalling the provisions they'd used and the laundry that Elena had done, he went into the kitchen and stocked a box with new supplies. He found the neatly folded stack of clean sheets, towels and borrowed clothes in the laundry room.

A few minutes later he was on his way. With the roads no longer hazardously covered with ice, the trip took less than a half hour. He pulled the car onto the shoulder alongside the creek and set out on foot. The full moon made the path through the cottonwoods easy to follow.

It took two trips to get everything to the line shack. Once inside, with the door closed behind him against the bitter wind, he felt the cabin's peaceful spell begin to weave its way around him again. Memories came flooding back, images of Garrett's face glowing with passion, of her provocative touches, her sweet kisses. Joshua groaned as need rocketed through him. Damn the woman for captivating him! Any other woman on earth would have been less trouble. Any other woman would have meant less confusion, less heartache.

No other woman would have done.

Not ready to let go of the memories just yet, he started the fire and took off his jacket. He made a pot of coffee, then began putting the supplies away and remaking the bed.

When the cabin was once again as they had found it on that night that had sealed their fate so firmly in his heart, he sat on the sofa and stared at the crackling flames. He thought of his fancy apartments, his expensive furnishings and realized this simple place, after just that one night, felt more like home to him now. Because of Garrett. In his mind, on that night they had become a family, husband and wife in every way that counted. No ceremony would unite them any more meaningfully. If only he could make her see that.

He touched the flannel shirt she'd worn that night, the one that had skimmed and revealed and taunted. The fabric was softer now and smelled of something sweet, something not nearly as sensual as Garrett. With a sigh, he slid down and rested his head against the back of the sofa. He rubbed a cuff of the shirt against his cheek and wondered again how something so right could be turning out so wrong. He still hadn't come up with an answer by the time he fell into a fitful sleep.

Garrett's nerves felt as if they'd been rubbed raw. Every noise, every creak of the house, every roar of the wind made her sit up and stare around the room, looking for who knew what.

Hoping for Joshua.

Finally, after a restless, impossible hour, she gave up. She dressed, went to the barn and saddled Bright Lightning. The horse was as eager as she to race the howling wind. It had been a long time since she'd ridden, a long time since her thoughts had been uncomplicated and her heart still her own. She would reclaim herself with this night ride, free herself from the memory of Joshua. She had no idea where she was going. She only knew she didn't want to be here in the morning when Joshua packed up his things and left. One goodbye was all she could take.

The full moon spilled a silver path before her. As if lured by the promise at the end, she gave Bright Lightning her head. The filly galloped at a fierce pace, flying across the land until both horse and rider were breathless. The hard ride should have exhausted Garrett, but she felt exhilarated. Her blood pounded. Her cheeks were stinging, her muscles aching. She felt totally alive. The last time she had felt quite this way had been in Joshua's arms, astride his supple body.

With a sigh she leaned forward in the saddle and rested her head against Bright Lightning's neck. "Damn," she murmured. She had chased away the blues but not the memories. If anything, with her heart thudding and the horse beneath her, thoughts of Joshua burned hotter than ever.

With a light touch of the reins, she found herself turning toward the Rutgers's line shack. Maybe if she confronted the past weeks head-on, she could put this mistaken interlude in her life to rest.

She approached the cabin from the east. Tethering Bright Lightning outside, she was almost to the door when she noticed that the snow around the front door had been trampled. A trail of footprints led back toward the highway. She followed them for a bit, until she caught a glimpse of that silly, impractical convertible of Joshua's. Her heart seemed to still.

"Why can't I get away from him?" she murmured to no one in particular. She started to go. She actually walked half a dozen paces toward her horse, giving the cabin a wide berth before being drawn back. She needed to know why he was here, why he'd sought refuge in this place. Was it for the same reason she had? Had he been seeking to banish memories once and for all? Or had he wanted to recapture them?

She found him asleep on the sofa, his head thrown back in a way that was bound to leave him with a stiff neck. His blond hair was mussed, his jaw shadowed with stubble. After only the faintest hesitation, she took off her jacket and sat beside him. It was only through sheer willpower that she confined herself to looking at him. She wanted desperately to touch, to soothe away the worried lines that creased his brow even in sleep. She wanted to know again the feel of his lips on hers. She wanted one last time to experience the wild joy of his caresses.

She denied herself all of that, telling herself it was wise, reminding herself that once imagined danger was now a painful reality. She curled her feet under her and watched the rise and fall of his chest. When she could finally bear it no longer, she dropped a light farewell kiss on that faintly crooked nose that reminded her of all the contradictions in his personality. She stood up and reached for her jacket again when his eyes blinked open.

"Garrett," he said, his voice husky with sleep. "I was just dreaming about you. I dreamed you kissed me."

Her lips curved just a bit. "I did. Just a peck, mind you."

He reached out a hand. "Would you kiss me again? I'd like to remember it while I'm gone."

She shook her head, heart hammering. "I don't dare."

"Why?"

"It would hurt too much. I ache inside, Joshua. I ache for what we're losing."

"Then hold onto it. Come with me in the morning. See how I live."

"You know I can't do that. I have responsibilities here."

A light seemed to go out in his eyes. He stood up and went to the fireplace, knelt down and stirred the embers until the dying sparks re-ignited. The action seemed fraught with symbolism. It made the ache even more painful to bear. Her nerves felt more raw now than when she'd lain alone in her bed only dreaming of Joshua.

"Maybe I should go," she said.

"No. Stay with me, please. Let's talk this out."

She shook her head. "If I stay, we won't talk."

Understanding flared in the depths of his eyes. He came back and sat beside her on the bed. "Maybe that's even better. Maybe that's the way we communicate best about what is really in our hearts."

"Making love is not an answer."

"Are you so sure of that?" he asked, his hand against her cheek. "Are you?" The back of his fingers rubbed against the hollow of her neck, then trailed lower until his hand stroked over her breast. The nipple tightened into a hard, sensitive bud. The shock seemed to cut all the way through her. He took her hand and pressed it to his lips. "Why did you come here tonight?"

"I can't explain it. Something drew me here."

"As it did me. Doesn't that tell you something, sweetheart?"

She stared at him helplessly. "I don't know. Maybe. Joshua, I don't know what to say to you anymore."

"And I don't know what to do anymore."

Their gazes caught and held. An eternity slid by...or maybe it was no more than a heartbeat.

"Just hold me," Garrett begged at last, not strong enough to deny herself this one simple pleasure. "Would you mind doing that? Suddenly I'm feeling very much alone and you haven't even left yet."

With a sigh, he drew her into his arms. With the fire crackling in the fireplace and his arms tight around her, Garrett felt safe and secure. If only the feeling would last, if only she could count on it being this way tomorrow and the next day and the next...

She stared up into eyes that had suddenly gone smoky with desire. His gaze lingered on her lips, then slowly he lowered his mouth to hers in a sweetly tender kiss. Hunger exploded inside her like a flower bursting into full bloom. She was the one who deepened the kiss, who turned it from a gentle caress into an urgent claiming. All of the longing she had kept at bay over the last days went into that one lingering kiss. Fire leapt in her veins. Her pulse hammered. Somewhere deep inside, doubts fled, if only for this moment, this one last time.

Joshua's hands were gentle, too gentle. She wanted him to rush, to send her flying with all the brightness of fireworks in the night sky. He insisted on savoring, on lingering over each kiss, exploring with exquisite care. Her skin warmed under his touch, her blood pulsed to an excited rhythm. Each caress was a bitter-sweet reminder that it was the last time she would know this joy, the last time she would know the aching, deep-down pleasure of a kiss, the heart-stopping thrill of his heat deep inside her.

Ironically, when time speeded up, when each thrust of his body lifted them higher and higher toward a shattering climax, Garrett wanted him to wait, wanted this sweet joining to go on forever. Her body, slick with perspiration and desperate with need, betrayed her, arching into his, catapulting her over the edge, drawing him with her.

Joshua's hands cupped her face and he stared deep into her eyes. "I love you." Each word was spoken emphatically, convincingly.

"I know," she whispered. "I know."

He sighed and rolled away. "But it's not enough, is it?"

Suddenly chilled by his anger, she trembled. "I don't know. I just don't know anymore."

"Garrett, I don't know what else to say, what else to do."

"You sound as if you're blaming me, as if I'm the one at fault because I can't give up everything to do this your way. That's not fair," she said.

"Not a damn thing about this is fair. And, yes, I'd like to know whose fault it is, if not yours. I've done everything I could think of to prove myself to you, to offer you a life that most women would envy."

The accusatory tone was still there and it filled Garrett with guilt. Uncomfortable with the emotion, she lashed back. "Maybe the bottom line is that you don't love me enough, either," she accused. "You're still trying to buy me."

"How can you say that? I've asked you to marry me. Isn't that proof enough?"

"No," she said. "No."

She climbed out of bed, away from the temptation of his body, away from the danger of her own responses. Grabbing her clothes, she jerked them on haphazardly. Unable to meet his condemning gaze, she stood in the doorway and whispered goodbye. Then, when it seemed certain he wouldn't respond, she closed it.

Only when she was safely on the other side, tears streaming down her face, did she dare to murmur, "I love you, Joshua. I really love you."

And then she ran.

Chapter Fifteen

Garrett raced from the cabin in a near panic. Suddenly she desperately needed the solace of home. She needed to remember what she was trying to protect, all that was important in her life. Riding back toward the ranch at a breakneck pace, she tried futilely to flee the power of the last stolen hour in Joshua's arms. Shaking and breathless when she arrived, she finally calmed as she curried Bright Lightning. Over and over she reassured herself that what had just happened didn't really matter, that she would survive Joshua's leaving in the morning and go on as before.

When the filly was bedded down in her stall, Garrett went outside. She leaned against the corral fence and stared at the night sky. The Big Dipper tilted clearly toward the North Star. Enthralled as always by the thick sprinkling of stars across the black-velvet backdrop, she barely heard the whisper of sound behind her, the faint crunch of ice-topped snow, yet she felt Joshua's presence. She supposed that in her heart she had known he would come after her, that he would never leave well enough alone. Tension crept through her as she waited, listening to his approaching footsteps, dreading another confrontation, another goodbye.

Then he was beside her, silent and still in a way that might have been comforting if his mere presence didn't so often set off such conflicting emotions. Irritation easily slipped into blazing anger. Fury too often slid into fascination and a pull so strong she was shaken by the implications. It had happened again tonight, even though he'd told her he was leaving, even though she knew it was over between them. Not since the night Casey had been conceived had she been so tempted to lose herself in the fool's-gold promise of a man's love. That had been a girl's misguided infatuation, though, while what she felt now was a woman's longing. The difference and her unwilling acknowledgment of it scared her to death.

Joshua was losing patience, losing the will to fight for her. She had heard the defeat in his voice. For weeks he had been content to let the heat build again, waiting until she shattered like a ceramic figure that had been fired too hot. Her resolve was close to shattering now and she hoped to God he didn't know it.

She wasn't sure she could withstand the pressure he was likely to put on her.

"Have you ever had a dream?" she asked, breaking the silence.

"All the time."

The quick, easy response told her he didn't understand. "No, I mean a dream that consumes you, that determines who you are and what you'll become."

She caught the faint shake of his head and sighed. "Then I'm not sure you could ever understand."

"Make me understand. You said earlier that you ache. So do I. I see how much we have and I see it slipping away. Tell me about your dream."

"From the time I was a little girl I dreamed of nights like this. I read *Little House on the Prairie* and longed to live like that, on the edge of a frontier, in a land with clean air and vivid blue skies and endless horizons, a place of limitless possibilities."

"What about the hardships?"

"They seemed like nothing compared to the hell I was living in," she said simply.

"What hell?" he asked. "Can't you please tell me now? Can't you trust me to understand? If I have to give you up, at least I need to understand why."

Garrett wanted to do as he asked, but she was afraid it would be like unleashing a tidal wave, that once started, the hurt and anger would never cease pouring out of her. She lifted her gaze to meet his and saw the kindness that underscored everything Joshua did. More than that, she saw the love. Taking a deep breath, she began, drawing strength from the fingers that laced with hers.

"By the time I was five we were crammed into a one-bedroom apartment on Chicago's south side. Our view was an alley. I slept on a sofa in the living room, along with my sister. My brother slept on the floor. He would wake up screaming, terrified that the cockroaches were crawling over him."

A shudder ran through her. "God, it was awful."

"Surely there was someplace else…"

"Yes," she confirmed flatly. "There was someplace else, but it made that apartment seem like heaven. It was a room down the hall from a crack dealer. All of us in that one dreary room."

"Oh, baby," he murmured, his voice thick with emotion. "Your parents, didn't they…how could they…"

She recognized his struggle to grasp reasons that after all these years Garrett herself didn't understand. Parents were supposed to love. They were supposed to protect. Hers hadn't. In a way they'd still been emotional children themselves, angry at life and totally self-indulgent.

Even though she had no valid explanation for the inexplicable, Garrett kept going, the words pouring out now. "After my father lost his job, he didn't give a damn about much of anything. My mother only cared about where her next bottle of booze was coming from. When I was eight, I was scavenging for food to keep my sister and brother alive. Every Christmas we'd get new clothes, castoffs really, from the church down the street. I hated those clothes. I hated knowing that even the fanciest dress with the prettiest lace and ribbons could make me a laughingstock because everyone would know that someone else wore it first. I wanted something new so badly it hurt. I did odd jobs, putting every extra penny I could get into a piggy bank, trying to save enough for a new pair of jeans. That's all I wanted, one damned pair of jeans." A bitter tear trickled down her cheek.

"Did you get them?"

"No. I came home from school one day and found my piggy bank shattered. My father tried to tell me we'd been robbed, but I knew better. Not even the most doped-up crack addict would bother robbing a dump like ours. Besides, there was a new bottle of liquor sitting on the table in front of my mother." She took a deep breath, then told him, "That was the day I vowed to get out. I stayed in school because it was the one place I could go and read. Books were my escape. The ones about the West were the best. The pioneers had such spirit, such determination. It seemed they could overcome anything. I wanted to be like that. I wanted to be strong."

Her voice dropped to a near whisper. "Then came Nicky."

"Casey's father?"

She nodded. "God, he was handsome. Thick dark hair. Midnight eyes. Strong features. He was gorgeous. And smart. And charming. He was twenty-two. I had just turned seventeen. We met in a restaurant, where I'd gotten a job as a waitress by lying about my age. He told me how beautiful I was. He bought me presents. He took me places I'd never been before, showed me a way of life I'd only imagined. I'd never felt so incredibly special in my entire life. It was just exactly like I'd read about in all the books. He was a real man, not like my father. Nicky was my knight in shining armor and I was being rescued. God, what a fool I was."

"You were seventeen years old, damn it."

"I should have known better, though. Men like that don't marry girls from the wrong side of the tracks."

"Men like me, you mean," Joshua said, his expression anguished.

She nodded. "Men like you," she agreed.

He winced at the accusation. She watched as he struggled for control. When he finally spoke, his voice was utterly calm. "What happened then?"

"I'm sure you can guess the rest."

"Tell me. I want to hear you say it."

It took every last bit of her bravery to admit, "Six months later I was pregnant and Nicky's parents were offering to buy me off."

She felt Joshua tense beside her, though his grip on her hand never wavered. His strength flowed into her. "What did he have to say about it?"

"He wouldn't see me. I was so sure they were keeping him away. God, it makes me sick when I think of the way I threw myself at him, begging him to talk to me, begging him..." Her voice caught on a sob. Drawing in a deep, calming breath, she went on. "When I finally realized that he'd never been in love with me, that I was only humiliating myself, I took their money and moved to Wyoming."

She lifted her gaze to Joshua's. "I came here with two things—a thousand dollars and the determination never again to be dependent on anyone. I've made a damned good life for Casey and for me."

"Yes, you have. You turned it around. Instead of letting what happened ruin your life, you made it the start of fulfilling your dream." He reached over and cupped her chin, turning her to face him. "Do you realize what kind of strength that took?"

She stared back at him unflinchingly and said quietly, "Do you?"

He held her gaze forever, then chuckled softly. "Message received."

"I hope so, Joshua. I truly hope so. I've worked damned hard for what I have. This beautiful place. My wonderful daughter. A rewarding job. I take none of it for granted and I won't give it up."

"I'm not asking you to give it up. I'm only asking you to share it."

"Oh, Joshua. It sounds so simple, but you know it's not that easy."

"Isn't it? Can't you do that much at least? Can't you let me become a part of the life you've created here? Marry me and let me replace all those painful memories with new ones, happy ones."

A beat passed, then another. When she didn't reply, he upped the ante. "I'll even move out here, if that's what it takes."

She wanted to believe in him, to grab at his offer to live here, but she could hear the reluctance in his voice. She wanted so much to accept his promise to be there for her always, but too many people had let her down. First her parents. Then Nicky. She didn't dare take a chance, didn't dare risk everything she had. And she couldn't ask him to give up a place he loved to live here with her. Finally she shook her head. "I can't. The past has a way of repeating itself."

"I'll never hurt you," he promised. "I won't let anyone hurt you again."

"I'm the only one who can do that."

"By keeping this wall around you?"

"Yes, if that's what it takes."

"And what about Casey?"

Garrett frowned at the question. "Casey is just fine."

"Is she? Then why does she have so many unanswered questions about her father? Have you ever told her what you just told me?"

"It would break her heart to know her father didn't want her."

"I'm sure she's already guessed as much. It's the uncertainty that really hurts her. Maybe that's none of my business, though. She's your daughter and you have to decide what she deserves to know. It is my business that the bond that was growing between Casey and me was deliberately broken. I will never understand why you felt the need to do that.''

''Because she needs to know she shouldn't count on anyone.''

''No,'' he said. ''Casey knew she could trust me. In her heart, she believed in me from the very beginning. You're the one who planted the seed of distrust in her mind. Is that your way of protecting her? Will you let her grow into a lonely, frightened woman like her mother?''

As the harsh words sank in, Garrett shuddered. She thought of her lovely, beautiful, gregarious daughter living the kind of hard life she had chosen for herself.

As if he knew that he'd struck home, Joshua said, ''Just think about it, Garrett. Think about how much you're robbing from Casey. Think of your daughter, if you won't think of yourself.''

And then he walked away, leaving her with her bitter memories and her shattered dreams. Tonight, through Joshua's eyes, she had seen the two twisted somehow into one sad, painful vision of an endless, lonely future.

For weeks after Joshua had gone, Garrett went around in a daze. She was moody and irritable. It was Red who finally snapped her out of her self-pity.

''Seems to me you're wasting time,'' he said, lounging in the big leather chair beside her desk.

They had spent the day going over reports and making decisions about marketing the cattle. There were fence repairs to be made, as well. Garrett's mind was on all of that, so it took a few minutes for her wandering attention to shift gears. "Sorry," she apologized. "I know I've been distracted lately."

"If you ask me, what you've been is lovesick. Ever since Joshua went back east, you've been looking like you've lost your last friend. Why don't you marry the man and put us all out of our misery."

"You know how I feel about marriage."

"Of course, I do. You told me every time I was fool enough to ask you. Course when it was me doing the asking, it made some sense. You never had a thing for me, the way you do for that greenhorn."

"Joshua is not a greenhorn," she defended automatically.

"About as close as a man can get. Never mind, though. That isn't the point. Why are you being so mule-headed, when you know it's what you want?"

"Habit," she said slowly, realizing as she said it that it was a good measure of the truth. The gut-wrenching fear that had kept other men at bay no longer applied when it came to Joshua. She knew in her heart he could be trusted. As he'd said, Casey had felt it instinctively and he'd proved it time and time again.

"A danged fool habit, if you ask me."

Her spirits suddenly began to soar. "It is, isn't it?" she murmured. Suddenly she was on her feet, flinging her arms around the startled foreman.

"Whoa," he said, setting her away from him. "You're hugging the wrong man."

"But you're the one who made me see what's been

in front of my face all along. Now how the devil do I show Joshua that I'm ready to take the next step in our relationship?''

''You might consider calling him.''

She thought of all the inventive ways he'd found to court her and shook her head. ''Too boring.''

''I doubt the man's looking for fireworks. A simple *I do* would probably suit him just fine.''

She grinned as her plan began to take shape. ''There's more than one way to get the message across.''

Red's eyes narrowed. ''You going to Florida? I could manage around here for a while, if that's what you've a mind to do.''

''Thanks, I'd really appreciate it. I promise not to be gone long.''

''Still say you could settle things mighty quick with a phone call. Let him foot the bill for the plane ride.''

She grinned. ''But what would the fun be in that? I'm going for something he'll remember for the rest of his life.''

''Suzy, where the hell's the damned report?'' Joshua shouted, prowling around the confines of his office. The wall-to-wall spread of glass facing the ocean did nothing to ease his claustrophobia or to soothe his frayed temper.

''Suzy?'' he bellowed.

The door opened a crack and Cal stuck his head in.

"Is it safe to come in or has this been declared a war zone?"

Joshua ran his fingers through his hair, then gestured Cal in. "I suppose Suzy would tell you to enter at your own risk."

"Having a bad day?"

"A bad month."

"Still no word from Garrett."

His gaze shot to Cal. "How did you know about that?"

Cal rolled his eyes. "You couldn't possibly be that dense. The phone lines between Wyoming and Ocala have been burning up since the minute you hightailed it away from the ranch with us. Marilou vowed if I didn't drive over here today to talk to you, she was coming herself. Having been the target of one of her well-intentioned campaigns, I thought I'd better save you the grief."

Joshua's irritation rose. "Are they all blaming this on me? I'm not the one who said no. I asked the woman to marry me, flat-out begged her, even if it meant having to give up all this and live in that god-forsaken hellhole. That sacrifice alone ought to tell you exactly how serious my intentions were."

"Were?"

"Are. Hell, I don't know anymore. The woman has the stubborn constitution of a mule. Maybe she's right. Maybe I am a lousy bet. Maybe all men are lousy bets."

"I take exception to that on my behalf and yours.

You've avoided marriage for thirty-seven years. I seriously doubt that you're going to change your lifestyle on some whim. You must be in love."

"Tell that to Garrett."

"As a matter of fact, I have. So has Marilou. So has my grandmother. Apparently so has Casey. My grandmother says Casey's threatened to move to the main house if her mother doesn't marry you. She must be feeling pretty ganged up on by now."

Joshua sank into his chair. "See what I mean? The woman is hopeless."

"She loves you, though, right? There's no question in your mind about that?"

"She loves me. I'd bet my entire stock portfolio on it and you know how seriously I take that."

"Then get yourself back out there and wear her down. Prove it to her. Open an office and relocate your headquarters. Buy a house. Hell, buy some cattle."

Joshua's eyes widened in horror. "Are you out of your mind?"

Cal grinned. "I don't think so. Can you imagine a better wedding present for a woman who's always dreamed of owning her own spread? Put it in her name. Let her know that it'll be hers, no matter what happens between the two of you in the future, that she'll have her security and her independence."

"In other words, buy her."

"A cynic might see it that way. A romantic wouldn't."

"I have never, in my entire life, met anyone less romantic and more cynical than Garrett."

"Joshua, are you blind? Experience has taught her that. Give her new experiences. A little wining and dining. I thought you were an expert."

"She doesn't trust my motives."

"Because you haven't made the one, grand gesture that could convince her. Make the commitment to Wyoming and a life with her, a commitment she can see, and her doubts will vanish."

Joshua shook his head. "And if they don't?"

"If I know you, you'll turn the ranch into the biggest cattle operation in Wyoming and sell it at a tidy profit. You can't lose."

The idea began to hold a certain appeal. It was just quirky and dramatic enough to convince her. "Are you smart enough to dream this up on your own?"

Cal chuckled. "Are you kidding? No man thinks this deviously. Grandmother and Marilou say it's a surefire solution."

"I don't suppose your grandmother knows of a cattle operation that's on the market," he said wryly.

"As a matter of fact," Cal said, drawing some papers from his back pocket, "here's the prospectus on a place she thinks would be just about perfect. It came by express mail this morning."

As Joshua scanned the papers, his eyebrows rose in disbelief. "This is half the damned state."

"I think it's the part Grandmother doesn't already own."

"I don't suppose she has any advice on financing."

"Well..." He handed over a mortgage application with her banker.

"She doesn't miss a trick, does she?"

"You don't get to be one of the most powerful ranchers in the state by not going after what you want."

"Is there a message in there for me, as well?"

"Could be, my friend. Could be."

Joshua folded the papers and tucked them into his briefcase. "Suzy!"

The secretary peeked around the door, but refused to set foot in the room. "It's safe," he told her. "Book me on the first flight back to Cheyenne."

"Take my plane," Cal offered. "It's fueled and waiting."

"I hate your pilot. He still thinks he's flying war missions."

"He is fast."

Now that he'd made up his mind, speed was a consideration. And Cal's plane did have a phone in it. With any luck he could wrap up the negotiations for the land en route and present the deed to Garrett within a few hours after his arrival.

"Make sure there's plenty of Scotch on board," he told Cal. "I may need it, especially if there's another damned foot of snow on the ground."

"Done. Good luck, my friend."

"Something tells me I'm going to need it."

An hour later he was in the air and on the phone.

The owner of the property was anxious to retire and get away to someplace warm. Joshua thought of his condo in Florida. If he was going to do this, there could be no looking back.

"I may have a solution for you there," he said. Twenty minutes later they had a deal.

"Damn, this better work," he muttered as the phone rang.

"Hey, boss, how's the weather up there?" Suzy inquired.

"Smooth. Anything happening I need to know about?"

"Does the fact that your office is filled with white roses mean anything?"

"White roses?" he repeated weakly.

"At last count there were twelve dozen and they're still coming. The florist seems a bit confused that he's not actually decorating a hotel ballroom for a wedding. Wait a sec. Someone new just came in and this one's not bearing flowers."

His head reeling, Joshua waited for more. The roses had to be from Garrett. No one else would understand the significance. But why so many? Why now?

"Boss, how do you feel about champagne?"

"Champagne?"

"A *lot* of champagne. Cases of champagne. Are we throwing a party that I didn't know about? Whoops, here comes a caterer."

Suddenly Joshua burst out laughing. The message was growing clearer by the minute. Somehow Garrett had finally realized that grand gestures and lavish gifts were only that, an attempt to please, an attempt to deliver a message that couldn't always be put into words.

"Boss, is this someone's idea of a joke?" Suzy asked.

"No, hon, I don't think it's a joke at all. I think it's deadly serious."

"Ohmigod!"

"What now?"

"There's a woman standing here in a wedding gown. Boss, are you sure you didn't forget something really, really important?"

"Is she beautiful?"

"Breathtaking," Suzy confirmed. Her voice dropped. "She looks nervous, though."

"I can just imagine," he said with another chuckle.

"What should I tell her?"

"Tell her I'm negotiating a deal and I should be back in the office in an hour."

"An hour?" Suzy squeaked.

"Not even kamikaze Joe here can fly this jet any faster than that. Don't let her out of your sight, Suzy. And if there's not a preacher and a marriage license arranged for this surprise party, get 'em. Pull whatever strings you have to."

"Should I call Mr. and Mrs. Rivers and tell them to get over here?"

Still grinning, Joshua said, "Something tells me they'll already be on their way."

Chapter Sixteen

Garrett felt like an idiot. From the minute she'd walked through the door to Joshua's office and had seen what twenty-five dozen roses looked like when amassed in one place, she wondered if she'd gone just the tiniest bit overboard. Mrs. McDonald, however, had urged her to go for broke. Over Garrett's objections, she had insisted on footing the bill, claiming that she'd foolishly missed out on her own daughter's wedding and had every right to make up for it with Garrett's. She'd taken over the arrangements with the logistical expertise of a military commander and the enthusiasm of a mother of the bride. Garrett hadn't had the heart to slow her down.

Now, though, with cases of champagne being

opened and trays of food being displayed on any available surface, all adding to a distinct air of unreality, she wondered if she should have set some limits. The wide-eyed expression on Joshua's secretary's face confirmed that nothing quite like this had ever happened in this office before. Not that that was particularly astonishing, she conceded. Weddings didn't usually take the groom totally by surprise.

If there was a groom, she thought, suddenly filled with apprehension. What if Joshua had lost patience with her? What if he'd decided to get on with a life that didn't include her? Or, almost as bad, what if he was out of town?

"You must be looking for Mr. Ames," the secretary said, following her hushed phone conversation. Though there was a definite twinkle in her eyes, her expression was outwardly impassive, as if brides turned up on the doorstep every day looking for her boss. "I'm Suzy Winters. You must be Garrett."

"How did you know?"

"I can't think of another woman he knows who would dare this. Can I help you?"

Garrett swallowed hard. "Is he here?" she asked, disgusted at the squeak in her voice. She certainly didn't sound very daring.

"Afraid not. He's at a meeting away from the office. He should be back within the hour, though. Could I get you something while you wait? Champagne, maybe?" A smile dashed across her lips, then retreated behind her businesslike facade.

Garrett chuckled. "It's a little too much, isn't it?"

"With a man as dense as my boss can be, you might as well hedge your bets."

Sensing an ally at once, Garrett nodded. "That was my thinking, too. Subtlety doesn't exactly sink in with him. Half the time I couldn't even get through to him with a direct hit."

"Are you expecting a minister? A few guests?"

Garrett nodded. "I told everyone to be here at three. I figured that would give me time to revive Joshua if he fainted dead away. It would also give me time to call it off if he told me to get lost."

"Somehow I don't think that's going to be his response. How'd you do it, by the way?"

"Do it?"

"Lasso him? Women all over the world have been trying for years. He's been resistant."

"I haven't the vaguest idea," she admitted, sinking down in a chair, the full skirt of her wedding gown spreading out around her. Mrs. Mac had personally picked out the dress, insisting that even an unorthodox wedding should observe some traditions. She'd spent an hour at the hotel fussing over the lace until Garrett had been ready to snap her head off.

Just then the florist, still clucking over the lack of suitable places to display his exorbitantly priced roses, came out of Joshua's office. He practically clicked his heels together as he presented her with his bill. Garrett looked at the total and swallowed a gasp. As she reached in her purse for her credit card, Suzy spoke up.

"Let me put them on Mr. Ames's account."

"One surprise today is probably enough," Garrett said, handing over the card. "I don't want the man to have a heart attack. Besides, my boss is taking care of everything and loving every minute of it. The woman is a closet romantic. I had no idea until I mentioned my plan to her."

"Given half a chance, I think most women are."

Moments later, inside Joshua's office, Garrett signed off on the bills for the catering and the champagne. Though the amount staggered her, it was mere pocket change to Mrs. McDonald. Garrett was uneasy with the sense of obligation implied, but for once in her life it didn't seem to matter. The only thing that mattered was showing Joshua how much she loved him. If it took a dramatic, outrageous gesture like this to do it, it was well worth the expense and the obligation.

She explored the office, studying what she could still see of the modern Scandinavian furniture. The crisp, clean lines and functional designs fit Joshua's no-nonsense personality. Buried under a sea of fragrant roses, however, the room had taken on a decidedly sensual personality that also fit. Hoping to calm her jittery nerves, she inexpertly popped the cork on a bottle of champagne sending a fizz of bubbles into the air.

The champagne tickled her nose, but did nothing for her nerves. She glanced at her watch. It was nearly three now. What if he didn't get back before the minister and the guests started arriving? Would he ever forgive her for putting him in the awkward position of having to give her his answer in front of witnesses, especially if that answer turned out to be no?

She heard the outer door open then close, and prayed it was Joshua. She clenched her hands together and waited. And waited. Maybe he'd been warned by the obviously loyal Suzy and had taken off again. Garrett opened the office door and peeked. A tall, red-faced man dressed in a suit and cowboy boots stood toe-to-toe with the diminutive Suzy.

"Where the devil is he?" he demanded, running his hand through a shock of prematurely white hair. "I've had this appointment for six weeks. First he was gallivanting around the country..."

"He was working on a client's account in Wyoming," Suzy corrected firmly.

"Whatever. All I know is I have a three o'clock appointment with the man and it's just about that now. Where the devil is he?"

"I've had to cancel all of his appointments for this afternoon, Mr. Schaeffer. I'm terribly sorry. I know Mr. Ames will want to see you as soon as possible, but something came up today that couldn't be helped. I did try to call you before you left your office to save you the trip. Perhaps, if you had checked for messages..."

Garrett grinned at the deft way in which Suzy had turned things around so that the man no longer seemed quite as certain that Joshua was the one at fault. His sunburned face turned one shade redder.

"I ain't gonna do business with a man I can't count on," he blustered. "I don't care if the recommendation came from the good Lord himself, it's no way to run an operation."

Garrett sensed that Mr. Schaeffer was about to bolt and it would be all her fault. Since she had no idea how valuable a client he might become, she threw open the door and stepped into the foyer. Startled, the man took a step back, his shrewd gaze taking in the wedding gown with an air of disbelief.

"Well, I'll be damned," he said softly. "Ain't you the prettiest little thing."

"Thank you," Garrett said, reassured by the compliment. Mrs. Mac had said the same thing, but she hadn't trusted it coming from her biased lips. "Forgive me for eavesdropping, Mr. Schaeffer, but I couldn't help overhearing about your cancelled appointment. I'm afraid it's my fault."

"How's that?" he said, obviously intrigued.

Garrett had met enough mavericks in her time to recognize one. Whatever business acumen Mr. Schaeffer might have, he was at heart an adventurer.

"I'm afraid I showed up without warning," she said, playing to that spirit of adventure.

"You running away from a wedding or something?"

"Actually, I'm here for a wedding."

"Here?" he said, looking around the reception area.

She gestured toward Joshua's office. "In there actually. I'm sure Mr. Ames would have given you more advance notice about changing your appointment, but he wasn't aware of my plans.''

His gaze narrowed suspiciously. ''You're gonna marry the man and he don't even know it.''

She smiled. ''That's about it.''

''Well, I'll be. Mind if I stick around to see how things turn out? This'll sure be something I can tell the missus about. She thinks business is dull.''

''As long as you don't hold it against Joshua for cancelling your appointment.''

''Hell, no. In fact, if those contracts were ready, I'd sign 'em this minute. I'm gonna enjoy doing business with the two of you.''

''Actually, I don't work here. I'm a cattle rancher.''

''Well, don't that beat all. So am I. How about we just go inside and talk till that fiancé of yours gets here.''

Roswell Schaeffer had a lot to say and talking made him thirsty. Garrett was very glad she'd ordered lots of champagne. In fact, she was beginning to feel less edgy by the time they'd started on the second bottle. Mr. Schaeffer was actually a very funny man. Or maybe it was the champagne. Her blood seemed to be singing with it. She was just thinking how agreeable the sensation was, when the door opened.

''What's this?'' Joshua inquired.

To her amazement, his attention seemed to be riveted on Roswell Schaeffer, not the roses, the food or her wedding gown. ''I can explain,'' she said.

"Could we have a little privacy?" Joshua asked the other man, never once looking at Garrett.

Mr. Schaeffer grumbled about missing out on all the fun, but he got to his feet and headed for the door.

"Please don't leave," Garrett said, suddenly feeling the need for an ally in case this didn't go at all the way she planned.

"I'll be waiting just outside," he promised her, then came back and leaned down to whisper, "A man'd have to be a fool to turn you down."

Her lips curved into a shaky smile. "Thanks."

When he'd gone, Joshua finally looked at her. At once his eyes darkened with familiar desire. "You look...stunning," he said in a low voice that slid over her nerves and set them aflame.

Clenching her hands together, she stared at him. "You're not surprised, are you?"

He shook his head. "I was on the phone with Suzy when you made your grand entrance. I was terrified you'd change your mind and leave before I could get back."

"Where were you?"

"In a plane."

"In the air?" she said incredulously.

He nodded. "Fortunately it was Cal's plane. The pilot turned it around."

"But where were you going? Was there some sort of emergency? Mr. Schaeffer had an appointment. Suzy said she'd cancelled it, that she'd had to cancel all of them. I thought it was because of me."

"No. Actually, something came up earlier."

"If it was that important, though, why did you come back?"

"I couldn't very well miss my own wedding, could I?" he said, smiling.

"We could postpone it," she offered, working to hide her disappointment. "I mean, if you were going someplace really important, I wouldn't want to interfere."

"Oh no you don't. I'm not about to risk having you change your mind again. Besides, how long can it take to say *I do?* We can go together."

"Combine your business with a honeymoon? Are you sure you won't mind?"

"Sweetheart, there is nothing, *nothing,* more important to me than marrying you. I'd almost given up on talking you into it. What finally convinced you?"

"I realized that I'd just gotten into the habit of saying no all these years and that all the things I'd worried about for so long didn't apply to the way we feel about each other. I spent too many years without anyone in my life. It didn't seem to matter before because I had Casey and Mrs. Mac and Red, but Red made me see that they would never be able to substitute for what you and I have together. I couldn't stand the thought of losing that feeling again, not just because I was being too bullheaded to take a chance."

"I owe this to Red, huh?"

She grinned at the note of possessiveness that had

crept into his voice. "Maybe you'll be a little more civil next time you run into him."

"If this works out the way I want it to, I won't be running into him all that often."

Garrett's heartbeat slowed. Surely after all that he'd said, he didn't intend to ask her to leave Wyoming after all. As much as she loved him, she wasn't sure she could bear that. "What do you mean?" she asked.

Joshua's fingers brushed across her lips. "Stop frowning. It's not what you think."

"What do you mean, then?"

He drew a bundle of papers from his pocket and handed them to her.

"What's this?"

"Your wedding present. I was on my way to Wyoming to finalize the deal when Suzy told me you were here."

Garrett spread open the contract and started to read. "It's a ranch," she breathed softly.

"It's yours, if you want it. In your name, no matter what happens in the future."

Tears spilled down her cheeks as she threw her arms around him. "Thank you," she whispered as his arms closed around her.

"No, thank you," he said solemnly.

"But I haven't done anything for you."

"You came here. You arranged this wedding. That's the most precious gift you could have given me. Your trust."

She lifted shining eyes to meet his. "We're going to make it work, aren't we?"

"If you can figure out a way to warm up the winters in Wyoming, we'll do just fine."

She grinned at him, fitting her body provocatively to his. "Oh, I have a few ideas about that."

She heard his breath catch and felt his pulse begin to race. "Is it working?" she murmured.

"Working? In another ten seconds I'm going to have to adjust the air-conditioning or embarrass us both in front of our wedding guests."

Just then the intercom on his desk buzzed. Keeping Garrett pressed close, Joshua leaned over and punched the speaker button. "This better be important, Suzy."

"There are half a dozen people out here wondering if they should go or stay."

His gaze dropped until it locked with hers. "What do you think? Want to hold out for a church wedding with all the trimmings?"

Garrett glanced around the room. "That would be far too ordinary for the two of us, don't you think?"

"You're turning into a regular little daredevil on me, aren't you?"

She nodded slowly. "I think I like it, too. I never felt safe enough before. You've given me that."

"Then you want to go for it now?"

"Let's do it."

There were sparks of delighted amusement in Joshua's eyes as he gathered her into his arms and planted a kiss on her lips. "We are going to have one hell of an adventure, sweetheart. I promise you that."

Unconcerned with the sudden arrival of Casey, Mrs. Mac, Cal and Marilou, Garrett sealed their bargain with a sizzling kiss of her own. "I can't wait," she murmured in his ear.

"That's an even better vow than *I do*," he told her, laughing. "I can't wait, either."

"Then let's get on with it," Casey said impatiently. She tugged on the minister's hand. "Do it quickly, before they change their minds."

Garrett reached out a hand to her daughter, whose eyes were shining with happiness. "Would you be my maid of honor, baby?"

"Oh, wow," Casey breathed, taking her place beside Garrett. She leaned around her mother and winked at Joshua. "I told you we could pull it off."

He winked back and Garrett's heart sang. This was the real gift he was giving her, this intangible feeling of love and family and commitment. Even if the deal on the ranch were to fall through tomorrow, she finally knew deep in her heart she would have everything she'd ever dreamed of.

* * * * *

RETURN TO WHITEHORN

Silhouette's beloved **MONTANA MAVERICKS** returns with brand-new stories from your favorite authors! Welcome back to Whitehorn, Montana—a place where rich tales of passion and adventure are unfolding under the Big Sky. The new generation of Mavericks will leave you breathless!

Coming from Silhouette Special Edition°:

February 98: LETTER TO A LONESOME COWBOY by Jackie Merritt

March 98: WIFE MOST WANTED by Joan Elliott Pickart

May 98: A FATHER'S VOW by Myrna Temte

June 98: A HERO'S HOMECOMING by Laurie Paige

And don't miss these two very special additions to the Montana Mavericks saga:

MONTANA MAVERICKS WEDDINGS
by Diana Palmer, Ann Major and Susan Mallery
Short story collection available April 98

WILD WEST WIFE by Susan Mallery
Harlequin Historicals available July 98

Round up these great new stories
at your favorite retail outlet.

▼ Silhouette®   Look us up on-line at: http://www.romance.net

Coming this December 1997 from

Silhouette SPECIAL EDITION®

*AND BABY
MAKES THREE:
THE NEXT
GENERATION:*

*The Adams women of Texas
all find love—and
motherhood—in the most
unexpected ways!*

The Adams family of Texas returns!
Bestselling author **Sherryl Woods** continues
the saga in these irresistible new books.
Don't miss the first three titles in the series:

In December 1997: **THE LITTLEST ANGEL** (SE #1142)
When Angela Adams told Clint Brady she was pregnant, she
was decidedly displeased with the rancher's reaction. Could
Clint convince Angela he wanted them to be a family?

In February 1998: **NATURAL BORN TROUBLE** (SE #1156)
Dani Adams resisted when single dad Duke Jenkins claimed
she'd be the perfect mother for his sons. But Dani was
captivated by the boys—and their sexy father!

In May 1998: **UNEXPECTED MOMMY** (SE #1171)
To claim his share of the White Pines ranch, Chance Adams
tried to seduce his uncle's lovely stepdaughter. But then he
fell in love with Jenny Adams for real....

Available at your favorite retail outlet.

Silhouette®

FIVE STARS
MEAN SUCCESS

If you see the "5 Star Club" flash on a book, it means we're introducing you to one of our most STELLAR authors!

Every one of our Harlequin and Silhouette authors who has sold over 5 MILLION BOOKS has been selected for our "5 Star Club."

We've created the club so you won't miss any of our bestsellers. So, each month we'll be highlighting every original book within Harlequin and Silhouette written by our bestselling authors.

NOW THERE'S NO WAY ON EARTH OUR STARS WON'T BE SEEN!

OVER
5 MILLION
BOOKS SOLD
SPECIAL OFFER INSIDE

 HARLEQUIN® Silhouette®

Welcome to *Love Inspired*™

A brand-new series of contemporary inspirational love stories.

Join men and women as they learn valuable lessons about facing the challenges of today's world and about life, love and faith.

**Look for the following April 1998
Love Inspired™ titles:**

DECIDEDLY MARRIED
by Carole Gift Page

A HOPEFUL HEART
by Lois Richer

HOMECOMING
by Carolyne Aarsen

Available in retail outlets in March 1998.

LIFT YOUR SPIRITS AND GLADDEN YOUR HEART
with *Love Inspired!*™

Steeple
Hill™

LI498

ALICIA SCOTT

Continues the twelve-book series— 36 Hours—in March 1998 with Book Nine

PARTNERS IN CRIME

The storm was over, and Detective Jack Stryker finally had a prime suspect in Grand Springs' high-profile murder case. But beautiful Josie Reynolds wasn't about to admit to the crime— nor did Jack want her to. He believed in her innocence, and he teamed up with the alluring suspect to prove it. But was he playing it by the book—or merely blinded by love?

For Jack and Josie and *all* the residents of Grand Springs, Colorado, the storm-induced blackout was just the beginning of 36 Hours that changed *everything!* You won't want to miss a single book.

Available at your favorite retail outlet.

Silhouette Books
is proud to announce the arrival of

A MOTHER'S GIFT

This May, for three women, the perfect Mother's Day gift is mother*hood!* With the help of a lonely child in need of a home and the love of a very special man, these three heroines are about to receive this most precious gift as they surrender their single lives for a future as a family.

Waiting for Mom
by Kathleen Eagle
Nobody's Child
by Emilie Richards
Mother's Day Baby
by Joan Elliott Pickart

Three brand-new, heartwarming stories by three of your favorite authors in one collection—it's the best Mother's Day gift the rest of us could hope for.

Available May 1998 at your favorite retail outlet.

WE KNOW YOU LIKED THIS ONE

Sherryl Woods is a fabulous author whose books are highly acclaimed by romance fans everywhere. Fellow author Heather Graham Pozzessere praises Sherryl Woods for her "warmth, wit and charm." We're sure after reading *Joshua and the Cowgirl* that you agree with the experts!

WE'RE POSITIVE YOU'LL LOVE THE NEXT BOOK FROM

Silhouette SPECIAL EDITION®

Our stars will only keep rising! Sherryl's next title will be just as good as her last—if not better. To make sure you don't miss it we're offering $1.00 off her next book or any Silhouette Special Edition book.

Look for *Unexpected Mommy*, Silhouette Special Edition #1171, available in May 1998 at your favorite retail outlet.